P9-CQQ-778

COOKING FOR JACK

COOKING FOR JACK

by Tommy Baratta
with Marylou Baratta

Introduction by
JACK NICHOLSON

POCKET BOOKS
New York London Toronto Sydney Tokyo Singapore

POCKET BOOKS, a division of Simon & Schuster Inc.
1230 Avenue of the Americas, New York, NY 10020

ISBN: 0-671-53560-9

First Pocket Books hardcover printing November 1996

10 9 8 7 6 5 4 3 2 1

Book design by LISA GOLDENBERG
Interior illustrations by EDWARD BRIANT
Jack Nicholson illustration by TOM BACHTELL

Printed in the U.S.A.

FOR JAMES BARATTA

ACKNOWLEDGMENTS

Thanks to my mother, who started me cooking early in life, and to my father, who taught me that an Italian man doesn't have to do the cleaning up.

Thanks to Judy, my wife of twenty-odd years, for being my one-woman cleaning crew while I was being creative in the kitchen.

Thanks to my sons, Jason, T. J., Michael, and Jack, and to Marylou's children, Kathy and Peter.

Thanks to the Pocket Books staff for all their hard work and enthusiasm: Sue Carswell, my editor *eccellente*, and Craig Hillman, her assistant *fantastico*; Gina Centrello, president and publisher; Kara Welsh, associate publisher; Emily Bestler, editorial director; Donna O'Neill, Brian Blatz, Lynda Castillo, Donna Ruvituso, Brian Heller, Paolo Pepe, and everyone else who helped pull this book off.

Thanks to Frank Weimann and Cathy McCornack at The Literary Group, to Carmel Berman Reingold, and to Diane Krakower, Valerie Sanchez, Larry Springer, and Annie Marshall for their invaluable assistance.

Heartfelt thanks to everyone at Marylou's Restaurant for their support and encouragement, and to Donny Soffer, a loyal friend with a big appetite.

And special thanks to my friend, Jack Nicholson, whose interest in and enjoyment of my cooking was the inspiration for this book.

CONTENTS

INTRODUCTION

by Jack Nicholson

I've played many different characters over the years—a hit man, a werewolf, a colonel, a jeweler—but one thing they've all had in common is that they all have been fed by Tommy Baratta. Until you've seen the wistful looks directed at my trailer door from hungry Hollywood professionals all hoping that Tommy's prepared enough extra food to rescue them from the caterer's table, you just don't know the power of this man's cooking.

It was in 1983, when we both were acting in *Prizzi's Honor*, that I first suggested to Tom that he cook for me, an offer I repeated on my next picture. I didn't think he'd say yes—he's always been so busy—but he did, and since then we've forged what, in my opinion, has turned out to be a very fine collaboration—him cooking, me eating.

One of the things I like about Tommy is that he doesn't call himself a chef. He's a cook, plain and simple, and it's this distinction that I think is emblematic of his entire approach to food. This is not to say that he can't cook with the best of them—he can—but he's also not afraid to experiment, to improvise in a pinch, to open up a can when fresh ingredients aren't available. While this fearlessness has occasionally led him astray (placing alligator meat on the menu, in one unfortunate instance), more often than not it has proved invaluable. A movie set is by no means a restaurant, and a film's shooting schedule can be unpredictable to say the least, but that hasn't slowed Tommy from producing delicious meals at all hours of the day and night. He's done everything from cooking linguine in the microwave in my hotel room to preparing an entire turkey dinner out in the middle of the woods. He's also "trained" several generations of personal chefs here at my home in Beverly Hills. (Having learned that my food edict is "Not Too Fancy," it's been Tommy's job to break it to these Cordon Bleu grads that no one's exactly going to be photographing their dishes.) Interestingly, at the same time he's done all this, he has also managed to run his own successful restaurateuring enterprises.

How does he do it? The simple truth is that Tommy knows food and loves to cook. There has never been a stove this man didn't approach with interest, or a kitchen that wasn't richer for his presence. Tommy also knows what foods taste best and what's healthy—which is important, since we're both what you'd call good eaters. The fact that I've been able to lose weight, love every bite of a meal, and be full afterward is testament to the Baratta touch.

I don't know where Tommy found the time to put this book together—I assumed he was busy cooking for me—but then one of Tommy's born-and-bred traits is that he knows how to keep his lip buttoned (*omertà*, doncha know), which is another reason we get along so well. Apparently he's had a change of heart, and this book is the result—secret recipes and all. Still, here's a little secret I bet he hasn't slipped into this book, and that I know is true: The backbone of his cooking style comes directly from his mother, Vera. And for my money, Vera's hot Italian peppers (which the good woman sends me in "care packages" every month) are worth their weight in gold.

While my own mother may not have passed along as extensive a culinary legacy to her son, she did have some sage advice when it came to cooking, and which I, in closing, am now passing along to you: "*Clean as you go.*"

Trust me, with this bit of kitchen wisdom, and Tommy's fail-proof recipes, you can't go wrong.

—Jack

Beverly Hills, 1996

Chapter One

IN THE BEGINNING...

PEOPLE ARE ALWAYS ASKING ME where and when I learned to cook. I think I was born knowing how. I come from a big Italian family where everyone cooked. One uncle owned a restaurant and many of our relatives were in the food service industry as owners and chefs. In our home and the homes of the rest of the family, the kitchen was always the center of activity. One person might be rolling out dough for pasta while someone else stirred a large pot of sauce and a third person was busy canning tomatoes.

As a kid, I went with cousins, uncles, and my father and grandfather to construction jobs out of town. We never went to fast-food places or the local greasy spoon for our meals; instead, we cooked for ourselves. The men knew how to make sauces for pasta and they taught us kids. If there was a farm nearby, it was even better: we bought fresh peppers, onions, tomatoes—whatever was available.

Freshness was everything, and aunts and uncles who had houses in "the country"—maybe 30 miles away from Brooklyn—grew their own vegetables on whatever large or small plot of land they had.

In the summer, long tables were set up in a grape arbor, and we feasted on salads of warm, ripe tomatoes and other just-picked vegetables. Pasta dishes—often made with fresh shellfish—would be followed by fresh chicken.

I learned that the secret of fine Italian cooking is to get the best ingredients and to do as little as possible to them. Basic flavors should not be hidden, and good food does not require fancy sauces.

As I grew older, dinners and parties were always at my house—whether I lived in New York or had a summer place on Fire Island or the Hamptons. I always had a crowd of people around me while I prepared meals in the kitchen.

With all that cooking expertise I could have become a professional chef, but instead I became a stylist for a number of television shows. After a successful career I decided to return to my first love, and my sister, Marylou, and I opened Marylou's Restaurant in Greenwich Village. But I enjoy a challenge and now I'm a restaurant and hotel consultant and I travel all over. I opened Mama B's Pizza Company and Harry's Diner in the Aventura Mall in Florida, and recently opened the Biz Bistro, a 250-seat Italian and French restaurant, also in Aventura. Having worked in television in the past, and co-owning a restaurant, I've met a lot of people in show business, and that's how I got to meet Jack Nicholson, to cook for him, and to write this book.

Jack and His Healthy Eating

Maybe you're asking yourself, "What does Jack Nicholson know about diets?" Like all actors, he knows plenty. One day he was told he had to look heavier to play Jimmy Hoffa, and then another time he was instructed to lose 20 to 30 pounds before he started shooting *Wolf*.

I've known Jack almost twenty-five years, and my cooking for him came about by chance. I was in Aspen, skiing, and I told Art Garfunkel to come over for supper.

"Can I bring Jack Nicholson?" he asked.

"Sure," I said.

I made gnocchi that night, a salad, and a pot of strong Italian espresso.

"Why can't I eat this way all the time?" Jack asked. "Simple food, tasty food." (He had three helpings of gnocchi, which I had made with tomato-basil sauce.) "Food that isn't all covered up with fancy sauces—but not boring either."

No one with an Italian background prepares boring food, and even before I started thinking "diet" I cooked with very little oil and no butter, but plenty of garlic, basil, crushed red pepper flakes, onions, and all kinds of hot peppers. Food big on flavor, but low on fat.

We got friendly over that gnocchi and subsequent dinners. "You ought to open a restaurant, Tommy," Jack would say, and then when he was starring in *Prizzi's Honor*, he suggested to director John Huston that I be hired as a consultant.

I knew plenty about the Brooklyn-Italian background that was featured in *Prizzi's Honor*, and Marylou says that if you look at Jack in that movie, you'll see that he's adapted his walk and speech to mine. John Huston also had me work with the other actors as a dialect coach, and then he gave me a part in the movie: I play the opera singer who appears at the party for the Don, played by Bill Hickey. And if that didn't keep me busy enough, I also prepared the food you see in the movie.

Jack invited me to stay at his house in Beverly Hills while they were shooting the movie, and it didn't take me long to find my way into his kitchen. That's how it began; since then I've spent about two months each year at Jack's house. I cook and show Jack's full-time chef how to prepare the meals that Jack likes best!

I owe a lot to Jack, and whenever I strayed from my culinary heritage and headed in the direction of French cuisine, Jack would say, "Not too fancy," and I would return to the low-fat, flavorful food that we both prefer.

I travel with Jack when he goes on location. The studios always arrange for a crew to provide meals—and they're good—but Jack prefers the food I make in his camper. These campers or trailers are like big mobile homes, complete with living room, dining area, bedrooms, bathroom, and a small kitchen. Meals have to be made quickly and at odd times—I never know when Jack is going to be between scenes—and they have to be filling as well as flavorful. Jack often works a twelve-hour day, and he couldn't make it on tea and toast alone.

I know Jack's favorite dishes, and they often become the favorites of other people on the set. Sometimes I prepare a pasta and fagioli or a thick vegetable soup, and the aroma wafts all over the place. When there's a break in the filming, there's a knock on the camper door and someone will be standing there with a clean coffee cup: "Tommy, can I have a taste? Do you have enough?"

When I cook, I always prepare more than enough. Whether I'm cooking for Jack in his trailer or home or at my house, I always make extra. I was brought up to be ready for unexpected company.

Besides, if there's anything left over, it's good for the next day, and many of my dishes can be frozen and used at another time.

When I first started cooking for Jack it had nothing to do with losing weight. He just liked the way I cooked and asked me to go on location with him. We both put on weight when we were doing *Hoffa*—I had a small part in that, too—and then he was told in 1993 he had to lose weight for *Wolf*. At that time I had been trying out low-fat cooking—a lot of what I did was based on information from the American Heart Association—and I decided I was 25 pounds overweight.

When I told Jack that I wanted to lose 25 pounds, he said, "Okay, I've got to lose about that for *Wolf*. How about cooking that low-fat stuff for both of us, and we'll both drop the pounds."

That was the start of my cooking low-fat, low-calorie dishes for Jack and me. Of the two of us, Jack is the more disciplined. I'm a hotel and restaurant consultant and a partner in my sister's restaurant, so when somebody says, "Tommy, taste this," I usually do. But when Jack goes on a program, he stays with it. And even though I fell off the diet wagon occasionally, I still managed to lose 25 pounds, as did Jack.

The easiest time was the first two weeks—each of us lost about 4 to 5 pounds per week. After that, weight loss slowed down. This is a pattern familiar to most dieters. The first 10 pounds are the easiest to lose, but it's important to stick to the plan even though your weight loss slows to 1 or 2 pounds each week.

Does my way of cooking work? It does—if you stick to my low-fat recipes. All diets work, but mine is not a diet, it's a way of changing your eating habits without depriving yourself. It's based on eating tasty food in healthy portions.

I see diets that call for eating an ounce of this or a teaspoon of that, and I know nobody can stick to a diet like that for long. You can't stay with a diet if you're hungry most of the time. That's why my recipes call for enough food to satisfy.

The pasta recipes, for example, call for either three quarters of a pound or a pound of pasta for four people—depending on the ingredients in the sauce. Jack and I can

eat a pound of pasta between us, and if I serve that much I make sure that the sauce is low in fat and calories—only 20 percent of each day's calories should come from fat.

I'm not suggesting you eat large quantities of food. A commercial cake manufacturer came out with fat-free pastries. Of course, they were loaded with sugar. A woman told me that she couldn't understand why she hadn't lost weight—sure, she ate an entire coffee cake for breakfast, but it was fat-free. The fat may have been low, but the calories were not, and you've got to watch out for both of them.

It's important to change your lifestyle. Get into the habit of watching what you eat and, at the same time, becoming more physically active. If you think about it, you'll realize that you don't burn up many calories through physical work. You don't even have to roll down a car window—just push a button. And who has to walk across the room to change a TV channel? Forget about it—just press the remote. We play a lot of golf, which helps, and Jack has a fully equipped gym in his house, which is great for workouts. A few laps in the swimming pool also burn up calories.

If you're not a golfer, swimmer, or tennis player and you don't belong to a gym, the next best thing is to walk. Twenty minutes a day, every day, is good. And if it's too cold or too hot to go outside—any excuse is good, right?—then follow one of those exercise programs on TV. There's one or more of them on just about every hour of the day.

Okay, want to be lean and mean like Jack Nicholson? Eat the way he eats, and cook the way I cook: low fat, low calorie, and loaded with flavor. Not to worry—you'll be able to follow every recipe in this book. Although I know about restaurants, this is not a book written by a restaurant chef who has a staff and every ingredient available to him, and who has studied at the Culinary Institute. This book is for the cook at home. I cook many of these dishes when I'm on location with Jack and I have to move fast and improvise, but still produce delicious meals—just like you, right?

Marketing

I go out on location with Jack whenever he's in a film. Those shoots can last anywhere from twelve to fourteen weeks, and the working days can be twelve hours or longer. Mealtimes are unpredictable—Jack may not be in the next two or three scenes, and something has to be ready for him to eat when he has the time.

Before the start of a movie, I make sure the camper is stocked with basics—some of the same basics you'll need in your kitchen if you want to prepare low-fat meals quickly and easily.

The following list contains a number of canned items. I can't always get fresh clams for clam sauce, and I don't have the time to rehydrate and cook beans for pasta and fagioli—that's why the camper shelves hold canned clams, bottled clam juice, and a variety of canned beans. Those canned items, and others, such as fat-free chicken broth, should have a place in your kitchen, too.

On location could mean that I'm in the middle of a desert or on top of a mountain or in freezing-cold Albany—which is where we were when we shot *Ironweed.* A grocery, supermarket, or butcher can be miles away; if you don't want to run to the store every time you're making a meal, take a look at my marketing list and use it as a basis for your own.

Here's what I keep in Jack's camper when I'm on location:

(Some of these ingredients are available to me only at the beginning of a shoot; you should be able to restock weekly.)

FRESH FRUITS AND VEGETABLES

Garlic
Onions
Potatoes
Tomatoes
Celery
Cabbage
Parsley
Bananas
Oranges
Apples

CANNED FOODS

Italian plum tomatoes
Italian crushed tomatoes
Fat-free chicken broth
Tomato paste
Clams
Clam juice
Beans: cannellini, chick peas, lentils, fat-free refried beans
Lentil soup
Tomato juice
Vegetable juice
Vegetable broth

IN THE FREEZER

Chicken cutlets
Italian bread
Baguettes
Low-fat muffins
Corn tortillas
Frozen yogurt
Peas
Spinach

IN THE REFRIGERATOR

Egg substitute
Nonfat ricotta
Nonfat mozzarella
Parmesan cheese
Low-fat mayonnaise

IN THE CABINET

Olive oil
Olive oil cooking spray
Vegetable oil cooking spray
Light soy sauce
Dijon mustard
Honey mustard
All-purpose flour
Flavored bread crumbs
Vinegar
Lentils
Salt
Peppercorns
Oregano
Crushed red pepper flakes
Bay leaves
Basil
Sugar
Vanilla
Hot cherry peppers in vinegar
Pickled vegetables
Variety of pastas
Hot salsa
Rice

Chapter Two

BREAKFAST

I'M A BELIEVER IN EATING a good breakfast. I know that the old-fashioned morning meals of bacon, eggs, and sausage are not for people watching fat and calorie intake, but I also know that you can't do a day's work when you start out with black coffee and a piece of toast. And believe me, actors work hard—their morning call can be as early as 5 A.M., and they stay on the set until 10 P.M. They're not in front of the camera the whole time, but they're on call, and while Jack has a large, completely outfitted camper, he's *on*, even when he's not on.

Since he has a long day before him, I prepare breakfasts that give Jack enough energy to keep going until the director calls a break either for lunch or to shoot a scene in which Jack is not involved.

The recipes in this chapter are good for breakfast or for a midmorning or midafternoon snack. I also prepare dishes that are not out-and-out breakfast foods: UNCLE AL'S POTATOES II (page 144), for example—a spicy combination of potatoes and hot cherry peppers—bring out the flavor of a low-fat omelette made with egg substitute and prepared in a nonstick skillet with a cooking spray. Look through the book—nothing wrong with serving chicken broth with tofu in the morning (page 55)—the Chinese and Japanese have been enjoying soups at breakfast time for years.

Basic Frittata

PER SERVING: FAT: 0.6 GRAM CALORIES: 146

Vegetable oil cooking spray
2 medium potatoes, cooked and cubed
1 small onion, finely diced
Egg substitute equivalent to 8 eggs
Salt and freshly ground pepper to taste
1 teaspoon grated Parmesan cheese
2 plum tomatoes, diced

Here's my basic frittata, which can be served for breakfast, brunch, lunch—or as a late-night quick feast. This recipe includes potatoes and onions, but I make frittatas with whatever I have in the refrigerator or pantry. Spinach, mushrooms, mustard greens, asparagus—a frittata can make any ingredients look and taste good. Once you know how to make a basic frittata—and it's easy—you'll always be able to put a meal on the table, even when unexpected company rings your doorbell or comes home with you after a late-night party.

1. Coat a large, nonstick ovenproof skillet with cooking spray.
2. Add potatoes and onion and cook over medium heat, stirring frequently, until potatoes are hot and onions are translucent.
3. Combine egg substitute, seasonings, and Parmesan cheese. Mix well and pour into skillet.
4. Cook over low-medium heat, raising edges of frittata to allow uncooked egg mixture into the bottom of the pan, until eggs are almost set.
5. Cover and continue cooking until eggs are set.
6. Place uncovered skillet in broiler and cook for an additional minute, or until top of frittata is lightly browned.
7. Transfer frittata to a serving platter and garnish top with tomatoes. Cut into wedges and serve.

Serves: 4

Twice-Baked Potatoes with Ham 'n' Eggs

PER SERVING: FAT: 2.4 GRAMS CALORIES: 307

*4 large baking potatoes**
1/4 cup skim milk
Salt and freshly ground pepper to taste
4 slices (about 4 ounces) Canadian bacon
Vegetable oil cooking spray
Egg substitute equivalent to 8 eggs
4 slices nonfat cheese, shredded

Marylou serves this as a brunch dish at our restaurant. But it's delicious anytime.

1. Bake potatoes until tender. Slice 1 inch lengthwise off the tops of the potatoes.
2. Scoop out potato pulp from shells into a small saucepan. Add milk and seasonings and mash over low heat.
3. Return about two-thirds of mashed potatoes to skins, pressing against shells, leaving a cavity. Discard remainder of potatoes, or save for another use.
4. Preheat oven to 350 degrees.
5. Cook bacon until lightly browned in a nonstick skillet. Sliver bacon, or cut into small cubes, and reserve.
6. Coat a nonstick skillet with cooking spray. Add eggs and scramble to desired degree of doneness.
7. Place bacon pieces into potatoes. Top with scrambled eggs.
8. Top eggs with shredded cheese.
9. Place potatoes on a cookie sheet or in a flat baking pan and bake until cheese has melted and ingredients are heated through, from 10 to 15 minutes.

   Serves: 4

*This dish may be prepared with leftover baked potatoes.

Banana Yogurt Muffins

Per serving (one muffin): Fat: 0.5 gram Calories: 129

Vegetable oil cooking spray
1 1/2 cups all-purpose flour
3/4 cup sugar
2 teaspoons baking powder
1 teaspoon baking soda
1/2 teaspoon salt
2/3 cup nonfat plain yogurt
2/3 cup skim milk
1 large, ripe banana, mashed

1. Preheat oven to 400 degrees.
2. Coat a nonstick muffin pan with cooking spray.
3. Combine all ingredients in a bowl. Whisk until all ingredients are just blended.
4. Spoon mixture into muffin pan.
5. Bake for 20 minutes, or until lightly browned. Serve immediately. (May be served with an all-fruit jam.)

Yield: 12 muffins

MORE ON FRITTATAS

My sister Marylou and I have a running argument about the chopped tomatoes that go on top of the basic frittata. I say the tomatoes should be lightly cooked and peeled and then chopped. Marylou likes the tomatoes unpeeled and uncooked. Now that I've told you that, the decision is yours. But Jack likes his tomatoes cooked—just thought you'd like to know.

Mexican-Style Breakfast

Beans are nourishing and filling, and when I know that Jack is going to have a really tough day I heat up a can of fat-free refried beans, put them in a corn tortilla, add scrambled eggs (made with egg substitute, of course) topped with shredded lettuce, and roll the tortilla. Serve lots of salsa on the side—the hotter the better, according to Jack.

STILL MORE ON FRITTATAS

A favorite dish of mine is pasta frittata prepared with cooked spaghetti. This is made by lightly sautéing 1 cup of cooked pasta in a skillet—with or without 2 slices of slivered Canadian bacon. Add the egg substitute, 1 teaspoon of grated Parmesan cheese, a couple of twists of nutmeg, and some chopped Italian parsley. Follow the directions for basic frittata, and if you wish, add a little chopped tomato—cooked—on top.

No Problem French Toast

PER SERVING: FAT: 3.3 GRAMS CALORIES: 194

Egg substitute equal to 4 eggs
1/2 cup skim milk
1 teaspoon vanilla
Pinch of nutmeg
Vegetable oil cooking spray
8 slices bread: may be cinnamon-raisin or Italian or French bread, cut diagonally into 1-inch slices
Maple syrup or RASPBERRY SAUCE (page 169)

1. In a bowl, combine egg substitute, milk, vanilla, and nutmeg. Whisk until blended.
2. Preheat oven to 200 degrees.
3. Coat a large nonstick skillet with spray and heat over medium heat.
4. Dip bread slices into egg mixture, until bread is saturated.
5. Sauté bread slices 2 minutes on each side, browning lightly. After bread is cooked, place in a shallow, nonstick baking pan or on a cookie sheet. Place pan in oven to keep toast warm.
6. Coat skillet after each batch is sautéed and repeat with remaining bread.
7. Place 2 slices of french toast on each plate and serve with maple syrup or raspberry sauce. (Sliced peaches may be substituted.)

Serves: 4

Chapter Three

APPETIZERS AND SMALL MEALS

I FIND THAT IT'S GOOD to have the ingredients in the house or in Jack's camper to prepare dishes that can be used as a first course or in combination to provide a small meal.

Salty, sugary, loaded-with-fat snacks are a tempting danger, but if you put together your own variety of small dishes you'll be less tempted to gorge on that bag of potato chips or chocolate candies.

When preparing appetizers, I always make extra AUNT MARGARET'S CAPONATA (page 38), which is great for snacking.

Stuffed Artichoke

PER SERVING: FAT: 2.7 GRAMS CALORIES: 174

4 medium artichokes
4 slices firmly textured white bread, trimmed
1 cup skim milk
2 tablespoons finely chopped flat, or Italian, parsley
Egg substitute equal to 1 egg
1 tablespoon grated Parmesan cheese
1 teaspoon olive oil
Salt and freshly ground pepper to taste
2 tablespoons lemon juice

1. Wash artichokes and, using a sharp knife, remove stem and cut 1 inch off the tops of the artichokes.
2. Trim off tough, outer leaves around the base of each artichoke. Reserve.
3. Soak bread in milk until just softened. Squeeze out excess milk and place bread in bowl.
4. Add all remaining ingredients, except for lemon juice, and mix thoroughly.
5. Working from the center, open leaves of artichokes and spoon stuffing between leaves.
6. Place artichokes in a skillet or shallow saucepan. Artichokes should fit closely against each other so that they do not tip over while cooking.
7. Add lemon juice and enough water to skillet so that liquid covers bottom third of artichokes.
8. Cover and bring to a boil. Reduce heat and allow artichokes to simmer for 45 to 50 minutes, or until a leaf is easily pulled from artichoke.
9. Using a slotted spoon, remove artichokes from liquid and drain. Transfer to a serving platter or 4 individual plates.

Serves: 4

Bruschetta with Tomatoes

PER SERVING: FAT: 4.6 GRAMS CALORIES: 301

1 1-pound loaf thin Italian bread, cut diagonally into 1-inch slices
2 garlic cloves, halved
3 large ripe tomatoes, chopped
1 medium red onion, chopped
3 tablespoons chopped basil
1 teaspoon olive oil
1 teaspoon oregano
1 tablespoon balsamic vinegar
Salt and freshly ground pepper to taste

1. Preheat oven to 350 degrees.
2. Place bread slices in one layer on a cookie sheet or flat baking pan and toast lightly on both sides.
3. Remove bread from oven and rub both sides with garlic. Reserve.
4. Combine all other ingredients in a bowl and mix thoroughly.
5. To serve, pass toast and tomatoes separately, or spoon tomatoes on bread slices before serving.

Serves: 4 to 6

Aunt Margaret's Caponata

PER SERVING ($^1/_4$ CUP): FAT: 0.7 GRAM CALORIES: 52

4 small Italian eggplant (about 1 pound)
Olive oil cooking spray
1 large onion, chopped
2 celery stalks, chopped
2 garlic cloves, minced
2 tablespoons capers
10 pitted black olives, sliced
$^1/_2$ teaspoon crushed red pepper flakes (optional)
1 teaspoon sugar
2 cups tomato sauce
2 tablespoons chopped basil
$^1/_4$ teaspoon cocoa powder
2 tablespoons balsamic vinegar

The secret of this terrific eggplant dish is the touch of cocoa powder that Aunt Margaret added to the ingredients. When everything is combined, there is no chocolate taste, but everyone who tastes this dish says, "What's in here? It's wonderful, but I can't figure it out."

I often double and triple this recipe because caponata is even better the second day and makes a great sandwich filling on a crusty baguette.

1. Peel eggplant and cube.
2. Coat a large skillet with cooking spray. Add eggplant and sauté for 5 minutes, stirring occasionally.
3. Add onion, celery, and garlic and continue sautéing for an additional 5 minutes.
4. Add capers, olives, red pepper flakes, sugar, and tomato sauce and cook for 5 minutes.
5. Stir in basil, cocoa powder, and vinegar. Cook over low heat for 10 minutes.
6. Transfer to a serving bowl. Caponata may be served warm or chilled.

Yield: About 2 cups

Codfish Cakes with Corn Salsa

Per serving: Fat: 0.9 gram Calories: 91

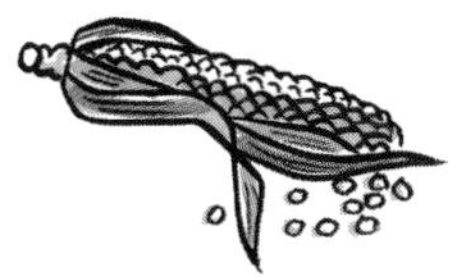

1 large russet potato, cubed
2 garlic cloves, halved
1 pound fillet of cod or scrod
Egg substitute equal to 1 egg
1/4 cup skim milk
2 tablespoons chopped flat, or Italian, parsley
Salt and freshly ground pepper to taste
3/4 cup homemade bread crumbs
Vegetable oil cooking spray
CORN SALSA (page 154)

1. Combine potato and garlic in a saucepan with a large amount of water.
2. Bring to a boil and cook for 10 minutes.
3. Add fish to potatoes and cook for an additional 10 minutes, or until potatoes are tender and fish flakes.
4. Drain and mash ingredients with a fork or potato masher.
5. Add egg substitute, milk, parsley, and seasonings.
6. Shape potato-fish mixture into 8 cakes and coat lightly with bread crumbs. Refrigerate for 20 minutes.
7. Coat a nonstick skillet with cooking spray.
8. Place cake in skillet and brown on each side. Serve with corn salsa.

Serves: 8

Crab Cakes

PER SERVING: FAT: 2.9 GRAMS CALORIES: 220

2 tablespoons nonfat sour cream
2 teaspoons dry mustard powder
1 teaspoon Worcestershire sauce
2 egg whites or egg substitute equal to 1 egg
1 cup plus 2 tablespoons finely crushed, fat-free saltine crackers
1 small onion, grated
1 tablespoon minced flat, or Italian, parsley
1/4 teaspoon hot sauce (optional)
Salt and freshly ground pepper to taste
1 pound lump crabmeat, shell and cartilage removed
Vegetable oil cooking spray
RED BELL PEPPER SAUCE (page 152)

1. In a large bowl, combine sour cream, mustard powder, Worcestershire sauce, 2 egg whites, 1 cup crushed crackers, onion, parsley, hot sauce, and seasonings. Mix thoroughly.
2. Add crabmeat and mix until all ingredients are combined. Mixture will be quite moist.
3. Form crabmeat mixture into 8 cakes and coat lightly with remaining cracker crumbs. Refrigerate for 20 minutes.
4. Coat a large, nonstick skillet with cooking spray.
5. Place cakes in skillet and brown on each side. If cooking in 2 batches, spray skillet again.
6. Serve with red bell pepper sauce.

Serves: 4

Peppers Stuffed with Rice

PER SERVING: FAT: 2.1 GRAMS CALORIES: 320

4 large bell peppers (any color)
1 cup rice
2 cups FAT-FREE CHICKEN BROTH (page 52)
Olive oil cooking spray
4 shallots, sliced
1/2 pound mushrooms, sliced
Egg substitute equal to 1 egg
2 tablespoons grated Parmesan cheese
Salt and freshly ground pepper to taste
1 cup fresh peas, or 1 10-ounce package frozen peas, thawed
2 cups tomato sauce (canned or homemade—page 157)

1. Preheat oven to 350 degrees.
2. Cut tops off peppers. Remove seeds and reserve peppers.
3. Combine rice and broth in a saucepan. Cover and cook until tender and liquid is absorbed, about 20 minutes. Reserve.
4. Coat a nonstick skillet with cooking spray. Add shallots and mushrooms and cook until mushrooms are just tender, stirring occasionally.
5. Transfer shallot-mushroom mixture to a large bowl. Add rice. Stir in egg substitute, cheese, salt, and pepper. Mix to combine. Fold in peas.
6. Stuff each pepper with rice mixture.
7. Coat the bottom of a casserole or baking dish with sauce. Place peppers in dish and pour remaining sauce over and around peppers.
8. Cover dish and bake for 20 minutes. Uncover and bake an additional 10 minutes.

Serves: 4

White Bean Dip

PER SERVING (1/4 CUP): FAT: 0.8 GRAM CALORIES: 69

2 cups cooked cannellini beans (if canned, drained and rinsed)
1 large garlic clove, cut in half
1 small onion, quartered
1 teaspoon olive oil
1/4 cup FAT-FREE CHICKEN BROTH (page 52)
Salt and freshly ground pepper to taste
1/4 cup chopped flat, or Italian, parsley

1. Combine all ingredients, except parsley, in a food processor.
2. Process until smoothly pureed.
3. Transfer bean dip to a serving bowl and stir in parsley. Cover and refrigerate until chilled.
4. Serve with raw vegetables, BAKED PITA TRIANGLES (page 148), thinly sliced Italian bread, or crackers.

Yield: Approximately 2 cups

Eggplant Spread

PER SERVING (1/4 CUP): FAT: 0.6 GRAM CALORIES: 24

1 large eggplant (about 1 pound)
1 small onion, quartered
2 tablespoons lemon juice
1 teaspoon olive oil
1 garlic clove
1/4 teaspoon Tabasco sauce
Salt and freshly ground pepper to taste
1 tablespoon minced flat, or Italian, parsley

1. Preheat oven to 375 degrees.
2. Using a sharp knife, prick eggplant in 4 or 5 places. (This is to prevent eggplant from bursting as it cooks, and turning the oven into a mess.)
3. Place eggplant in a shallow, nonstick baking dish and bake for 1 hour, or until eggplant is tender.
4. Remove eggplant from oven and cut in half horizontally.
5. Place eggplant halves in a strainer, flesh side down, and allow to drain for 15 minutes.
6. Scoop eggplant pulp from skin and place in a food processor. Add all remaining ingredients, except for parsley, and puree.
7. Transfer eggplant to a serving bowl and refrigerate until chilled before serving.
8. Garnish with parsley and serve with crackers or BAKED PITA TRIANGLES (page 148).

Yield: Approximately 2 cups

Lobster Roll

Per serving: Fat: 3.4 grams Calories: 221

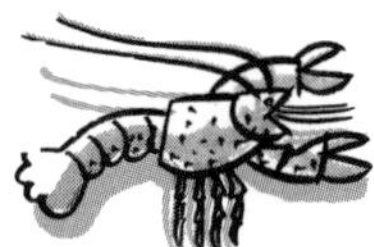

2 $1\frac{1}{2}$-pound lobsters, cooked
2 stalks celery, finely chopped
3 tablespoons low-fat mayonnaise
1 tablespoon nonfat sour cream
Salt and freshly ground pepper to taste
4 frankfurter rolls

1. Remove lobster meat from shells and cut into small pieces.
2. In a bowl, combine lobster, celery, mayonnaise, and sour cream. Mix until thoroughly combined and season to taste. Cover and refrigerate for 1 hour.
3. Warm or lightly toast frankfurter rolls. Split each roll open and fill with lobster salad just before serving.

Serves: 4

Oysters on the Half Shell Mignonette

Per serving: Fat: 2.3 grams Calories: 98

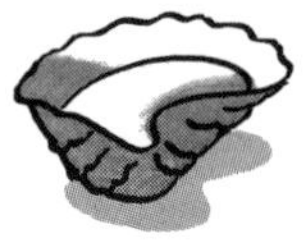

2 tablespoons red wine vinegar
2 tablespoons balsamic vinegar
1 tablespoon Worcestershire sauce
$\frac{1}{2}$ cup dry white wine
2 shallots, finely chopped
Freshly ground pepper to taste
24 very fresh oysters on the half shell
2 lemons, quartered

1. Combine all ingredients, except for oysters and lemons, in a bowl. Mix thoroughly.
2. Place 6 oysters on each of 4 plates. Spoon mignonette sauce over oysters and garnish each serving with lemon wedges.

Serves: 4

Shrimp and Ginger Wonton

PER SERVING (ONE WONTON): FAT: 0.4 GRAM CALORIES: 38

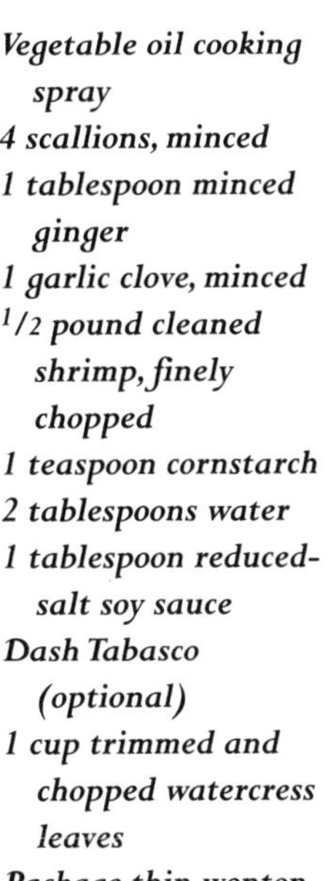

Vegetable oil cooking spray
4 scallions, minced
1 tablespoon minced ginger
1 garlic clove, minced
1/2 pound cleaned shrimp, finely chopped
1 teaspoon cornstarch
2 tablespoons water
1 tablespoon reduced-salt soy sauce
Dash Tabasco (optional)
1 cup trimmed and chopped watercress leaves
Package thin wonton wrappers

1. Spray a nonstick skillet with cooking spray.
2. Add scallions, ginger, garlic, and shrimp to skillet. Cook, stirring, for 3 minutes.
3. Combine cornstarch and water in a small bowl. Mix well and add to skillet. Stir to combine.
4. Add soy sauce, Tabasco, and watercress to skillet. Cook, stirring, for 1 additional minute. Remove mixture from heat and allow to cool.
5. Place 1 teaspoon of shrimp mixture in the center of a wonton wrapper. Moisten the edges of the wrapper with cold water. Fold wrapper into a half-moon shape and seal by pressing edges together. Repeat with remainder of shrimp mixture.
6. To cook, steam appetizers for 10 minutes and serve with dipping sauce.

Yield: About 20 shrimp and ginger appetizers

Shrimp and Cucumber Salad

Per serving: Fat: 1.5 grams Calories: 145

2 cucumbers, thinly sliced
6 scallions, thinly sliced
2 medium tomatoes, sliced
3 tablespoons chopped flat, or Italian, parsley
Salt and freshly ground pepper to taste
1/4 cup nonfat sour cream
1 tablespoon skim milk
2 tablespoons chopped dill
1 pound cooked medium shrimp, peeled and deveined
1/2 head Boston or Bibb lettuce, separated into leaves

1. In a bowl, combine cucumbers, scallions, tomatoes, and parsley. Season to taste with salt and pepper.
2. In another bowl combine all remaining ingredients except for shrimp and lettuce. Mix thoroughly and spoon over cucumber-scallion mixture. Toss gently.
3. Place lettuce leaves on 4 plates, spoon cucumber salad onto lettuce, and top with shrimp.

Serves: 4

Tuna and Bean Stuffed Tomatoes

Per serving: Fat: 2.9 grams Calories: 174

4 large ripe tomatoes
Salt and freshly ground pepper to taste
1 6-ounce can solid white tuna, water packed, drained
1 cup cooked and chilled cannellini beans or Great Northern beans
4 scallions, finely chopped
1 small red onion, thinly sliced
2 tablespoons finely chopped cilantro or parsley
1 teaspoon olive oil
2 tablespoons balsamic vinegar
2 cups baby lettuce greens

Everyone loves tuna—I know that Jack does. When he's between takes and only has time for a light lunch, this is the dish that I prepare. It tastes good, looks good, and takes minutes to fix.

1. Cut a 1/4-inch slice off the top of each tomato and reserve.
2. With a teaspoon, scoop out pulp from tomatoes and place in a bowl. Season tomato shells with salt and pepper and reserve.
3. Add tuna, beans, scallions, onion, and cilantro to tomato pulp.
4. Combine oil and vinegar. Mix well and pour over tuna combination.
5. Mix all ingredients and season to taste.
6. Spoon tuna mixture into tomato shells and top with reserved tomato slices. Place on a bed of baby lettuce greens and serve.

Serves: 4

Wilted Spinach Salad with Canadian Bacon

PER SERVING: FAT: 2.4 GRAMS CALORIES: 68

1 pound spinach, washed and trimmed
2 slices Canadian bacon, slivered
3 tablespoons balsamic vinegar
1 teaspoon extra-virgin olive oil
1 tablespoon honey
Salt and freshly ground pepper to taste

1. Dry spinach in a salad spinner or pat dry. Tear leaves in half and place in a salad bowl.
2. Heat bacon in a nonstick pan, turning frequently.
3. Remove from heat. Add vinegar, oil, and honey to pan and stir to combine.
4. Spoon bacon-dressing mixture over spinach and season to taste with salt and pepper. Toss to combine.

Serves: 4

Mussels Arinice

PER SERVING: FAT: 1.7 GRAMS CALORIES: 105

Olive oil cooking spray
2 garlic cloves, chopped
1 cup dry white wine
1 tablespoon Dijon mustard
2 pounds mussels, scrubbed and debearded
2 tablespoons chopped flat, or Italian, parsley
Lemon wedges
Freshly ground pepper

1. Coat a heavy saucepan or Dutch oven with cooking spray.
2. Add garlic and sauté over low heat for 1 minute.
3. Add wine and mustard and stir to combine.
4. Add mussels and cover. Cook over medium heat until mussel shells open, about 15 minutes.
5. Discard any mussels that have not opened. Spoon opened mussels with liquid into 4 bowls. Garnish with parsley and serve with lemon wedges and pepper.

Serves: 4

Chapter Four

SOUPS

MANY OF MY SOUPS are more than soup—they're often loaded with beans, vegetables, and pasta, and work out to be a three-course meal that's made in one pot. Soups can be filling, and this definitely works if you're watching fat and calories.

Soups have a lot going for them: most of them are served hot—good on a cold day—and they're comforting if you're feeling down, have a cold, or are just plain hungry.

I often serve Jack a salad, hearty soup, good bread, and dessert. And it is more than satisfying.

Fat-Free Chicken Broth

PER SERVING (ONE CUP): FAT: 0 GRAMS CALORIES: 33

4-to 5-pound stewing chicken, quartered, with giblets (not including liver)
2 stalks celery, coarsely chopped
2 carrots, coarsely chopped
1 medium onion, quartered
1 herb bouquet tied in cheesecloth: 4 sprigs parsley, 1 bay leaf, 1 teaspoon dried thyme, 1 clove garlic
1/4 teaspoon freshly ground white pepper

1. Rinse chicken and giblets thoroughly and place in a large soup pot. Add all remaining ingredients and enough water to cover ingredients by 2 inches.
2. Cover and bring to a boil. Reduce to a slow simmer and continue cooking uncovered. Skim and discard the gray foam that rises to the top after 5 to 10 minutes. Continue skimming. When there is no longer any foam, partly cover pot and continue cooking.
3. Cook for 2 to 3 hours, or until meat is tender when pierced with a fork. While cooking, add more water if necessary so that ingredients are always covered with water.
4. Remove all solid ingredients, discard vegetables and giblets, and set aside chicken. Strain stock into a large bowl and refrigerate. After broth has chilled, remove congealed fat from surface and discard.
5. To use chicken, allow to cool. Remove and discard skin. Cut meat from bones, discard bones, and use meat for salads or sandwiches.
6. Broth can be frozen for future use.

Yield: About 1 quart

Escarole Soup

PER SERVING: FAT: 0.6 GRAM CALORIES: 86

Olive oil cooking spray
2 garlic cloves, finely chopped
1 medium head escarole, coarsely chopped
1 quart FAT-FREE CHICKEN BROTH *(page 52)*
1 cup fresh peas or 1 10-ounce package frozen peas, thawed
Salt and freshly ground pepper to taste

1. Coat a soup pot with cooking spray.
2. Add garlic. Sauté for 1 minute, stirring frequently.
3. Add escarole. Cover pot and cook until escarole is wilted, about 5 minutes.
4. Add remaining ingredients. Cover and bring to a boil. Reduce heat and simmer for 5 minutes.
5. Transfer to a tureen and bring to the table, or ladle into 4 bowls.

Serves: 4

Creamy Carrot Soup with Basil

PER SERVING: FAT: 0.3 GRAM CALORIES: 128

2 bunches thin, young carrots, thinly sliced
4 cups FAT-FREE CHICKEN BROTH *(page 52)*
1/2 cup minced basil
1 cup nonfat sour cream
Salt and freshly ground pepper to taste
4 unblemished basil leaves

1. Combine carrots and broth in a soup pot. Bring to a boil.
2. Lower heat to a simmer. Cover and cook until carrots are tender, about 30 minutes. Add minced basil.
3. Transfer soup to a food processor and puree.
4. Return soup to pot and stir in sour cream. (Be careful not to let soup come to a boil.) Season to taste with salt and pepper.
5. Heat soup before serving and ladle into 4 bowls or soup dishes. Garnish each serving with 1 basil leaf.

Serves: 4

Broth-Tofu Pick-me-up

PER SERVING: FAT: 6.2 GRAMS CALORIES: 171

Vegetable oil cooking spray
8 wonton wrappers
4 cups FAT-FREE CHICKEN BROTH *(page 52)*
1/2 pound firm tofu, drained and cut into 1/2-inch pieces
2 scallions, thinly sliced
1 tablespoon minced cilantro

Sometimes late in the day you want *something* to eat, but you don't know what would appeal to you. Rather than another cup of espresso with a piece of cake, I fix this quick, filling soup and save many unwanted fat grams and calories.

1. Preheat oven to 375 degrees.
2. Coat a shallow, nonstick baking sheet with cooking spray.
3. Cut wonton wrappers into wide strips and place on baking sheet. Coat with cooking spray. Bake until lightly browned and crisp, about 7 to 10 minutes.
4. Combine broth and tofu in a saucepan or soup pot. Cover and bring to a simmer. Heat through. Stir in scallions and cilantro.
5. Ladle into bowls and serve with wonton noodles.

Serves: 4

Fusion Vegetable, Chicken, and Noodle Soup

PER SERVING: FAT: 8.1 GRAMS CALORIES: 780

2 quarts FAT-FREE CHICKEN BROTH *(page 52)*
2 cups dry white wine
1 tablespoon light soy sauce
2 tablespoons shredded ginger
Salt and freshly ground pepper to taste
2 medium carrots, thinly sliced
1 small cauliflower, separated into florets
1 small bunch broccoli, florets only
1 cup fresh water chestnuts, peeled and sliced (or canned water chestnuts)
1 pound small mushrooms, thinly sliced
1 pound snow peas, trimmed
1/2 pound green peas, shelled, or 10-ounce package frozen peas, thawed
1 chicken breast (about 1 pound), boned, skinned, and cut into strips
*1 pound fresh fettuccine**
1 tablespoon sesame oil

This dish combines Eastern and Western food ideas, which is why I call it fusion soup.

This is one of my favorite diet dishes: it combines vegetables—and I try to include these whenever I can—with protein from the chicken and carbohydrates from the noodles. It's also filling enough to take Jack through an afternoon of filming. It's really a whole meal that comes out of one pot.

1. In a large soup pot, combine broth, wine, soy sauce, ginger, and seasonings. Cover and bring to a boil.
2. Reduce heat to a simmer. Add carrots, cauliflower, broccoli, and water chestnuts. Cover and cook for 5 minutes.
3. Add mushrooms, snow peas, peas, and chicken. Cover and cook for 5 to 10 minutes, or until chicken is cooked. (Dish may be prepared in advance up to this point.)
4. Just before serving, return liquid to a boil. Add fettuccine and cook until *al dente,* about 3 minutes. Correct seasoning.
5. Stir in sesame oil and ladle into bowls.

Serves: 4

VARIATION: Shrimp, scallops, or pork tenderloin may be substituted for the chicken.

*If using dry pasta rather than fresh, cook the pasta separately and add to the soup bowls just before serving.

Herbed Corn and Potato Chowder

PER SERVING: FAT: 0.9 GRAM CALORIES: 202

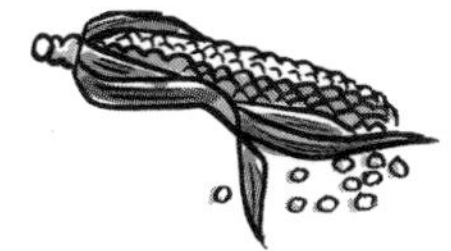

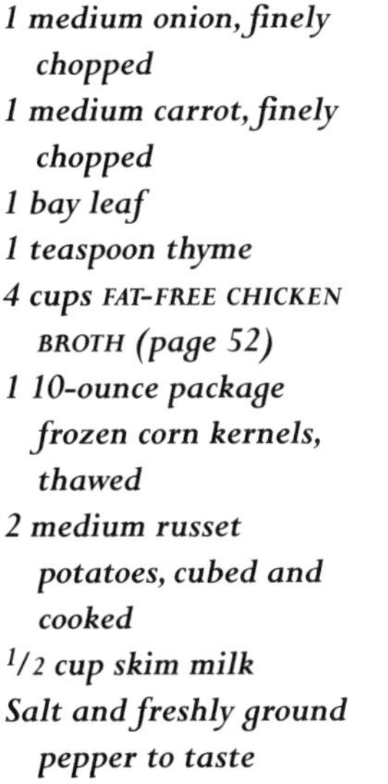

1 medium onion, finely chopped
1 medium carrot, finely chopped
1 bay leaf
1 teaspoon thyme
4 cups FAT-FREE CHICKEN BROTH *(page 52)*
1 10-ounce package frozen corn kernels, thawed
2 medium russet potatoes, cubed and cooked
1/2 cup skim milk
Salt and freshly ground pepper to taste
1/4 cup minced flat, or Italian, parsley

1. In a soup pot combine onion, carrot, bay leaf, thyme, and broth. Bring to a boil.
2. Reduce heat to a simmer. Cover and cook for 10 minutes.
3. Remove bay leaf and discard.
4. Add 1/2 package of corn and half the potatoes. Stir to combine.
5. Transfer soup to a food processor and puree. Depending on the size of your processor, you may have to do this in 2 or more steps.
6. Return soup to pot. Add remainder of corn and potatoes. Stir in milk and bring to a boil.
7. Reduce to a simmer. Cover and cook for 5 minutes. Season to taste with salt and pepper. Stir in parsley before serving.

Serves: 4

Melange of Fresh Vegetables

Per serving: Fat: 0.7 gram Calories: 199

1 medium onion, sliced
2 garlic cloves, chopped
4 scallions, chopped
2 carrots, sliced
2 medium potatoes, cubed
1 small head of cabbage (green or red), coarsely shredded
1 small zucchini, diced
2 small ripe tomatoes, quartered
2 tablespoons minced flat, or Italian, parsley
3 cups vegetable juice or broth
1 cup water
Salt and freshly ground pepper to taste
2 tablespoons minced dill

I wanted to prepare a light lunch one day, yet I didn't have anything ready. So I checked out the refrigerator and found an assortment of fresh vegetables.

I quickly peeled and chopped and combined the vegetables in a soup pot with vegetable juice and water. I added a bit of seasoning, and a short time later there was lunch—with the addition of thinly sliced, crusty Italian bread.

Don't be tied to the specific ingredients in the following recipe; feel free to add and subtract, using vegetables that I know you'll find in your refrigerator. This recipe calls for vegetable juice and water, but you can also use tomato juice, vegetable broth, or just water. Improvise! You can't go wrong.

1. Combine all ingredients, except for seasonings and dill, in a large soup pot. Liquid should cover vegetables; add more water if necessary.
2. Cover pot and bring liquid to a boil. Reduce heat and simmer until vegetables are tender, about 30 minutes.
3. Season to taste and stir in dill. Serve piping hot in large soup bowls.

Serves: 4

Potato Leek Soup

Per serving: Fat: 0.3 gram Calories: 146

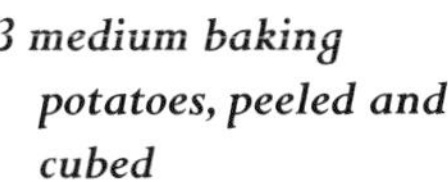

3 medium baking potatoes, peeled and cubed
2 leeks, white part only, thinly sliced
2 garlic cloves
4 cups FAT-FREE CHICKEN BROTH *(page 52)*
Salt and freshly ground pepper to taste
2 tablespoons minced flat, or Italian, parsley

1. Combine all ingredients, except for seasonings and parsley, in a soup pot.
2. Bring to a boil. Reduce heat and allow soup to simmer for 20 minutes, or until potatoes are tender.
3. Transfer solids with half of liquid to a food processor and puree. Return puree to soup pot. Season to taste with salt and pepper and heat.
4. Ladle soup into 4 bowls and garnish with parsley.

Serves: 4

Danny DeVito's Escarole and Bean Soup

PER SERVING: FAT: 1.2 GRAMS CALORIES: 187

Olive oil cooking spray
1 medium onion, coarsely chopped
2 garlic cloves, chopped
1 head escarole, coarsely chopped
1 quart FAT-FREE CHICKEN BROTH *(page 52)*
2 cups cooked cannellini beans
Salt and freshly ground pepper to taste

This is the dish that kept Danny going when we were shooting Hoffa in Pittsburgh in 1992. First of all, it was cold—very cold, and then Danny was doing double duty, directing and acting in the film—a lot of responsibility. The only time anyone saw him was when I prepared this dish. Danny would appear at the camper door with, "Tommy, you got any of that 'shcarole' soup for me?" This is really more than a soup—the beans make it a main dish—a healthy and satisfying way to keep going, especially on a cold day.

1. Coat a soup pot with cooking spray.
2. Add onion and sauté, stirring frequently, for about 3 minutes.
3. Add garlic and continue sautéing and stirring for 2 minutes.
4. Add escarole and cover. Cook until escarole has wilted, about 5 minutes.
5. Add broth and 1 cup of beans. Cover and bring to a simmer.

6. While soup cooks, puree remaining cup of beans in a food processor. Add bean puree to soup. Stir to combine.
7. Cover soup and simmer for 15 minutes. Season to taste with salt and pepper. Serve piping hot with crusty bread. To round out the meal you'll need nothing more than a salad and a dessert.

Serves: 4

COOKING BEANS

A number of my recipes call for cooked beans. If you use canned beans—and I find they work just fine—be sure to drain the beans, rinse them under cold, running water, and drain again before continuing with the recipe.

If you prefer cooking dried beans from scratch, here's the easiest way of rehydrating them: Put the beans in a large pot and cover them with 4 inches of cold water. Bring the water to a boil and cook the beans for 10 minutes. Remove the beans from the heat, cover the pot, and allow the beans to soak in the hot water for 1 hour.

Drain the beans and add cold water or other liquid to amply cover the beans. Cook over medium heat until the beans are tender. Depending on the age of the beans, this could take from 45 minutes to 1 1/2 hours. The beans should always be covered with liquid as they cook, and you can add garlic or an onion to the bean pot. Drain the beans when you're ready to use them.

On-Location Soup

Often a director will say, "Don't take too long for lunch. I want to finish shooting this scene and I don't want to lose the light."

I look into the fridge and I pull out a carrot, a celery stalk, and some garlic. If I don't have the carrot, that's okay, too. I heat a pan with some olive oil cooking spray and chop up the vegetables. I stir them around in the skillet for a couple of minutes and then throw in a can or two of lentil soup and some cooked pasta, which I always keep in the refrigerator coated with FAT-FREE CHICKEN BROTH (page 52). Heat the whole thing. Is it soup yet? You bet.

THE ELECTRIC HAND BLENDER

I'm not big on gadgets. I use a sharp knife more than any other kitchen tool. But, in addition to a food processor, which I use a lot, I've found that a small electric hand blender is a terrific appliance to have in the kitchen. When I want to puree soup right in the pot or prepare just a small amount of sauce, the electric hand blender is what I reach for. If your kitchen is not equipped with this handy tool, you might consider purchasing one; more good news—they're not expensive.

Onion Soup

Per serving: Fat: 4.1 grams Calories: 381

Vegetable oil cooking spray
6 large onions, thinly sliced
6 cups vegetable broth
1 bay leaf
2 ounces dry sherry (optional)
Salt and freshly ground pepper to taste
1/2 pound nonfat mozzarella cheese, shredded
4 1-inch slices of French or Italian bread, toasted

1. Coat a large soup pot with cooking spray.
2. Add onions and cook, stirring occasionally, over low heat until onions brown. Be careful not to burn onions.
3. Add broth, bay leaf, and sherry to onions. Cover and simmer for 30 minutes. Remove bay leaf and season to taste with salt and pepper.
4. Preheat oven to 375 degrees.
5. Sprinkle cheese over bread slices and reserve.
6. Ladle soup into 4 ovenproof bowls. Place one bread slice on top of each soup bowl.
7. Place a shallow baking pan or cookie sheet into oven and place soup bowls on pan.
8. Bake until cheese melts on top of bread slices and serve immediately.

Serves: 4

Pureed Bean and Vegetable Soup

PER SERVING: FAT: 0.7 GRAM CALORIES: 156

1 cup cooked cannellini beans
4 stalks celery, coarsely chopped
1 large onion, chopped
6 plum tomatoes, chopped
4 young small carrots, chopped
2 tablespoons chopped basil
4 cups FAT-FREE CHICKEN BROTH *(page 52)*
Salt and freshly ground pepper to taste

1. Combine beans, celery, onion, tomatoes, carrots, 1 tablespoon basil, and broth in a large soup pot.
2. Cover and bring to a boil. Reduce heat to a simmer and cook for 30 minutes.
3. Transfer soup to a food processor and puree. Depending on the size of your processor, you may have to do this in 2 or more steps.
4. Return soup to pot and season to taste with salt and pepper. Heat thoroughly before serving and garnish with reserved basil.

Serves: 4

Vermouth-Flavored Mushroom Consommé with Chives

PER SERVING: FAT: 1.7 GRAMS CALORIES: 86

Olive oil cooking spray
1 medium onion, minced
1 pound mushrooms, sliced
4 tablespoons sweet vermouth
3 cups vegetable broth
Salt and freshly ground pepper to taste
2 tablespoons chives

1. Coat a saucepan with cooking spray.
2. Add onion and mushrooms and sauté, stirring, over low heat for 2 minutes. Do not let ingredients brown.
3. Add vermouth and broth. Bring liquid to a simmer.
4. Cover and cook for 10 minutes. Season to taste with salt and pepper.
5. Garnish with chives before serving.

Serves: 4

Chapter Five

PASTA

THERE'S NOTHING EASIER than cooking pasta. All you need is a large pot, plenty of water, and—if you wish—salt. If you don't want the pasta to stick together, make sure that you bring 4 quarts of water to a boil for each pound of pasta. Some of my recipes call for 3/4 pound of pasta, and then you need about 3 quarts of water, but more water is better than less. If you have any fat-free chicken broth (page 52) around, or liquid from cooked vegetables, you can add them to the pot for a little extra flavor.

When the water comes to a boil, add salt. Wait for the water to return to a serious boil and add all the pasta. If you add the pasta gradually, it won't cook evenly. With a wooden spoon, occasionally stir the pasta as it cooks. This—and the large amount of water—will prevent the pasta from clumping.

Cook the pasta until it is just *al dente*—or firm to the bite. You want pasta with texture, not pasta that's overcooked and soft. How long should you cook pasta? I find the times given on pasta boxes not of much use; if you follow those directions, I think you'll end up with overcooked pasta most of the time.

No one can give you the exact cooking times for pasta—a lot depends on the size and shape. Thin spaghetti, for example, cooks much faster than penne or ziti. So stand by your pasta pot—the whole process takes only minutes—and sample as you cook. When the pasta is *al dente*, drain immediately and continue with the recipe. If the dish calls for sauce, have the sauce prepared before you cook the pasta. It's okay for the sauce to wait for the pasta, it's not so good for the pasta to chill and congeal as it waits for the sauce.

There's an old joke about how you can tell if the pasta is properly cooked: throw the pasta against the wall: if it sticks, it's overdone; if it bounces off the wall, it's not done; but if it sticks and then slides, it's done just right.

Now, how much pasta should you prepare for each person? Many diet recipes call for 2 ounces of pasta per person. My recipes call for 1/4 pound and only use less when combined with other ingredients. I don't believe that anyone sitting down to a meal will be satisfied with less, and an unsatisfied dieter will head for the refrigerator and food that is usually more loaded with calories than pasta. Besides, if you use a tiny amount of spaghetti today, and a small amount of fusilli tomorrow, your cupboard will be crowded with all those half-filled pasta boxes, and who wants that?

Mike Nichols's Penne with Tomatoes

PER SERVING: FAT: 6.5 GRAMS CALORIES: 515

2 pounds ripe tomatoes, coarsely chopped
2 large garlic cloves, sliced
1 bunch basil, coarsely chopped
Salt and freshly ground pepper to taste
1/2 pound Buffalo mozzarella, cubed (optional)
1 tablespoon olive oil
1 pound penne, cooked al dente
4 teaspoons grated Parmesan cheese

I met Mike Nichols at Jack's house, and he's eaten at Marylou's Restaurant many times. I make this penne for Mike when he comes to dinner. It's his favorite pasta dish, but it can be made only in the summer, when fresh tomatoes are at their absolute peak. Don't even try it in the winter, when tomatoes taste like cotton. The recipe can be made with or without wonderful, creamy and rich Buffalo mozzarella. If you're feeling good about your weight, add the cheese, but if you're not, this dish is delicious without it.

1. Combine all ingredients, except for the penne and Parmesan cheese, in a large bowl. Toss to combine.
2. Place bowl in the sun and allow flavors to meld. If the sun isn't available, allow tomato mixture to remain unrefrigerated for about 4 hours.
3. Place penne in a serving bowl. Top with tomato mixture and toss to combine. Serve with Parmesan cheese.

Serves: 4

Cavatelli with Broccoli Rabe and Sausage

PER SERVING: FAT: 5.5 GRAMS CALORIES: 384

Olive oil cooking spray
2 2-ounce links Italian turkey sausage, thinly sliced
1 garlic clove, minced
1/2 cup FAT-FREE CHICKEN BROTH (page 52)
2 bunches broccoli rabe
1/4 teaspoon crushed red pepper (optional)
1/4 cup dry white wine
Salt or freshly ground pepper to taste
1 pound fresh cavatelli, cooked al dente
4 teaspoons grated Parmesan cheese

Cavatelli, which are shaped like small, long shells, may be found in stores specializing in pasta or in the frozen food section of supermarkets.

1. Coat a large nonstick skillet with cooking spray.
2. Add sausage slices and brown lightly, turning frequently. Add garlic.
3. When garlic is translucent, add broth. Stir to combine and cook an additional 2 minutes.
4. While sausage cooks, separate broccoli rabe leaves from stalks. Discard stalks and wash leaves, allowing water that clings to leaves to remain.
5. Add leaves and red pepper flakes to skillet. Stir and cook 1 minute.
6. Add wine, salt, and pepper. Cover and cook for 5 minutes. If sauce seems too thick, add 1 or 2 tablespoons of water from pasta.
7. Place cavatelli in a serving bowl. Top with sausage-broccoli rabe mixture and toss to combine.
8. Serve with Parmesan cheese.

Serves: 4

Pasta Shells with Bean and Vegetable Combination

PER SERVING: FAT: 4.5 GRAMS CALORIES: 582

Olive oil cooking spray
1 large onion, finely chopped
2 whole scallions, sliced
4 garlic cloves, minced
2 red or yellow bell peppers, chopped
2 celery stalks, sliced
1 pound mushrooms, sliced
2 large ripe tomatoes, chopped
2 tablespoons chopped flat, or Italian, parsley
2 tablespoons chopped basil
Salt and freshly ground pepper to taste
1 teaspoon oregano
1 cup dry white wine
2 cups cooked cannellini beans
3/4 pound medium pasta shells, cooked al dente
4 tablespoons grated Parmesan cheese

1. Coat a Dutch oven with cooking spray.
2. Add onion and scallions and cook, stirring occasionally, for 2 minutes.
3. Add garlic and sauté for an additional 30 seconds.
4. Add bell peppers and celery and cook, stirring occasionally, for 2 minutes.
5. Add mushrooms, tomatoes, parsley, and basil and cook, stirring, for 1 minute.
6. Add salt, pepper, oregano, and wine. Stir to combine and cover. Cook over low heat for 15 minutes.
7. Drain beans in a colander. Rinse and drain again. Add beans to vegetable mixture. Cover, and cook an additional 5 minutes.
8. Place pasta in a serving bowl. Spoon sauce over pasta and toss to combine.
9. Sprinkle Parmesan cheese over pasta and serve.

Serves: 4

Penne with Cauliflower

PER SERVING: FAT: 2.7 GRAMS CALORIES: 516

1 medium head cauliflower
Olive oil cooking spray
1 small onion, thinly sliced
1 garlic clove, chopped
4 plum tomatoes, peeled and chopped
1/4 cup FAT-FREE CHICKEN BROTH *(page 52)*
Salt and freshly ground pepper to taste
1 pound penne, cooked al dente
1/2 cup seasoned bread crumbs

1. Steam cauliflower until just tender. After cauliflower has cooked, separate into florets and reserve.
2. Coat a large skillet with cooking spray.
3. Add onion and sauté for 1 minute.
4. Add garlic and sauté, stirring. Be careful not to let garlic burn.
5. Add tomatoes and cook for 5 minutes.
6. Add broth and seasonings and simmer for an additional 5 minutes.
7. Add cauliflower to sauce and toss to combine.
8. Place penne in a broiler-proof casserole. Top with cauliflower sauce and mix. (Dish may be prepared in advance up to this point.)
9. Before serving, sprinkle bread crumbs over pasta-cauliflower mixture and place under broiler until ingredients are heated through and crumbs have browned.

Serves: 4 as a main dish, 8 as a side dish (this is very good with chicken).

Whole Wheat Pasta with Celery and Smoked Chicken

PER SERVING: FAT: 5.0 GRAMS CALORIES: 547

Olive oil cooking spray
8 celery stalks, thinly sliced, leaves finely chopped and reserved
3/4 pound smoked breast of chicken, skinless, diced
2 cups FAT-FREE CHICKEN BROTH *(page 52)*
1/4 teaspoon crushed red pepper flakes (optional)
2 teaspoons cornstarch
1/4 cup dry vermouth
Salt and freshly ground pepper to taste
1 pound whole wheat pasta (any shape), cooked al dente

1. Coat a large skillet with cooking spray.
2. Add celery and sauté, stirring occasionally, for 2 minutes.
3. Add chicken and sauté for an additional minute.
4. Add broth and red pepper flakes. Cover and cook over low heat for 5 minutes.
5. In a bowl, combine cornstarch and vermouth. Mix to combine and add gradually to skillet, stirring. Cook until sauce has thickened and is clear. Season to taste with salt and pepper.
6. Place pasta in a serving bowl. Spoon sauce over pasta and toss to combine. Garnish with reserved celery leaves before serving.

Serves: 4

Thin Spaghetti with Crab Sauce

Per serving: Fat: 3.6 grams Calories: 538

Olive oil cooking spray
1 small onion, chopped
2 garlic cloves, minced
1/2 cup dry red wine
1 28-ounce can Italian crushed tomatoes
1 teaspoon oregano
1/2 teaspoon crushed red pepper flakes (optional)
2 tablespoons chopped basil
Salt and freshly ground pepper to taste
4 blue claw crabs, cleaned
1 pound thin spaghetti, cooked al dente

When I was a kid living in Brooklyn, on nice summer weekends the whole family would pile into my father's Packard and drive out to Long Island to visit an aunt and uncle who had a farm near the shore.

Late in the afternoon my aunt would say to my cousins and me, "Go catch some crabs for dinner."

We would gather up crab-catching equipment—square nets, ropes, and long poles with nets dangling from the end—and pile into an old jalopy. One of the men would drive us to the dock, saying he'd come back for us in a few hours.

We'd pick up scraps of fish to use as bait and either place them in the square nets or tie them to the end of the ropes. It didn't take long for the crabs to bite; we'd net them and dump them into burlap potato sacks. We had a fine time, and by the time one of my uncles came for us we'd have caught dozens of crabs.

Back at the house my aunt prepared a wonderful crab sauce, and as dinner time approached more and more cars piled with people would arrive. We gathered at a long wooden table set outside in the grape arbor—there were usually twenty or twenty-five of us. Soon my aunt and some of the other women would come from the kitchen bearing giant bowls of pasta over which my aunt had ladled the fragrant crab sauce. The crabs were placed on giant platters and we all helped ourselves. Everyone grabbed a crab, broke apart the shell, and picked out the meat.

And crabs weren't all that we ate. While the kids had been crabbing, some of the men had gone clamming, and the dinner table was covered with platters of clams on the half shell and clams oreganata. There were also salads and just-picked vegetables, fresh from the garden. Naturally, there was lots of crusty bread—but *never, ever* butter. Dessert was always fruit—usually a large watermelon, cold, just right after a huge meal. Often there were also peaches—picked from the trees that grew close to the house—and these had been sliced and marinated in homemade red wine. What a day we had—and what a dinner!

While I can't re-create that whole meal for you, I have managed an easy and delicious version of my aunt's wonderful crab sauce. This recipe calls for blue claw crabs, but one Dungeness crab may be substituted.

1. Coat a large saucepan or Dutch oven with cooking spray.
2. Add onion and garlic and sauté for 5 minutes.
3. Add wine, tomatoes, oregano, red pepper flakes, basil, salt and pepper, and crabs. Cover and simmer for 30 minutes.
4. Remove crabs from sauce. When cool enough to handle, crack shells and remove meat.
5. Return crabmeat to saucepan and simmer for an additional 5 minutes.
6. Place pasta in a serving bowl. Spoon crab sauce over pasta and toss before serving.

Serves: 4

Linguine with Clam Sauce and Spinach

Per serving: Fat: 6.0 grams Calories: 560

1 tablespoon olive oil
4 garlic cloves, finely chopped
1 cup dry white wine
Juice of 1/2 lemon
1 10-ounce package frozen spinach, thawed
1 cup bottled clam juice
1/8 teaspoon crushed red pepper flakes
1 8-ounce can chopped clams
2 tablespoons finely chopped flat, or Italian, parsley
1 pound linguine, cooked al dente

When I'm on location—and I've been on location in some strange places—I don't have the opportunity to search for a fine seafood shop when I want to prepare linguine with clam sauce. I'm usually working in a tiny kitchen in a camper and I've learned to cook with canned and frozen ingredients. The results are fine, but if you want to substitute fresh clams for canned, you may do so.

1. Heat olive oil in a large nonstick skillet.
2. Add garlic and sauté, stirring, until garlic begins to brown.
3. Add wine and lemon juice and cook over medium heat until ingredients are reduced by one third.
4. Add spinach, clam juice, and red pepper flakes. Bring to a boil and add chopped clams. Cook for 1 minute. Remove from heat and stir in parsley.
5. Place linguine in a bowl. Pour sauce over pasta and toss.

Serves: 4

Eggplant and Rigatoni

PER SERVING: FAT: 2.7 GRAMS CALORIES: 409

1 pound small Italian eggplant (about 4)
Olive oil cooking spray
3/4 pound rigatoni, cooked **al dente**
2 cups TOMATO-BASIL SAUCE *(page 157)*
3 tablespoons nonfat ricotta cheese
2 teaspoons grated Parmesan cheese
2 tablespoons chopped flat, or Italian, parsley

1. Preheat oven to broil.
2. Peel eggplant and cut into thin slices, lengthwise.
3. Place eggplant in one layer on a nonstick cookie sheet and coat with cooking spray.
4. Broil until lightly browned, about 3 minutes. Turn and broil on second side. Remove from broiler and reserve.
5. Place pasta in a bowl. Add sauce and toss.
6. Transfer pasta to the center of a serving platter. Spoon ricotta on top of pasta.
7. Arrange eggplant slices around pasta. Sprinkle all with Parmesan cheese and garnish with parsley.

Serves: 4

Basic Gnocchi

PER SERVING: FAT: 0.5 GRAM CALORIES: 248

4 medium potatoes (about $1^1/_2$ pounds)
1 cup (approximately) all-purpose flour
TOMATO-BASIL SAUCE (page 157), or
LOW-FAT PESTO (page 160), or
SPINACH SALSA (page 161)

Unless you have an Italian mother or grandmother in your family, your first attempts at gnocchi-making might end in a small disaster—if the dough is too soft, the gnocchi will dissolve in boiling water; if too hard, the result will be a dumpling that's tough. Now that I've said that, I think you should try it anyway because there's nothing as delicious as homemade gnocchi. Understand that the amount of flour in the recipe has to be approximate, because if the potatoes are a bit watery you'll need more flour. After a while, as you knead the gnocchi dough, your fingers will tell you when the amount of flour is just right, and you'll be happy with the results. Okay, here goes.

1. Boil the potatoes (without peeling) until tender. Drain. Allow potatoes to cool until you can handle them.
2. Peel and mash potatoes, making sure there are no lumps.
3. Place mashed potatoes in a bowl and add flour gradually.
4. Knead potato-flour mixture until dough is soft and smooth. Dough should be just stiff enough to hold a shape. Add flour as you work.
5. Place dough on a floured board and flour your hands. Form dough into rolls as wide as your finger, and cut into 1-inch pieces. Press each piece gently against the inside of a fork or against a floured cheese grater to vary the texture and create a design.

6. Bring 4 quarts of water to a boil and add about 20 gnocchi at a time. When the gnocchi come to the surface, remove from the pot with a slotted spoon and place in a serving dish. Moisten with a small amount of one of the sauces.
7. Repeat with remaining gnocchi and spoon sauce over all. (If using tomato-basil sauce, you may also sprinkle 4 teaspoons of grated Parmesan cheese over the gnocchi.)

Serves: 4

MARYLOU'S SECRET GNOCCHI RECIPE

My sister can make good gnocchi from scratch with the best of them, but there are times when her restaurant keeps her too busy and she has to take a few shortcuts at home. I'm about to reveal one quick idea that she's never told anyone before. If you're in a hurry and want to serve gnocchi, use instant mashed potatoes. They work just fine, and there's never a worry about lumps! Prepare the instant mashed potatoes with water rather than milk, and add flour. Knead the mixture until the dough forms and holds together. The gnocchi dough should be soft, but firm enough to roll. Follow the remaining directions for BASIC GNOCCHI (page 78-79).

Joe Pesci's Mother's Sweet Potato Gnocchi

PER SERVING: FAT: 0.8 GRAM CALORIES: 299

4 medium sweet potatoes (about $1^1/_2$ pounds)
$1^1/_2$ cups (approximately) all-purpose flour
4 quarts water
Serve with one of the following sauces:
LOW-FAT PESTO (page 160),
MUSHROOM-RICOTTA (page 85), or
RED BELL PEPPER SAUCE (page 152)

One day Joe Pesci came to dinner and asked, "Did you ever make sweet potato gnocchi?" When I said no, he suggested I call his mother, Mary, in New Jersey and ask for the recipe. I did, and I've been making sweet potato gnocchi ever since. It's one of my favorite dishes.

1. Boil the potatoes without peeling, until tender. Drain. Allow potatoes to cool until you can handle them.
2. Peel and mash potatoes, making sure there are no lumps.
3. Place mashed potatoes in a bowl and add flour gradually.
4. Knead potato-flour mixture until dough is soft and smooth. Dough should be just stiff enough to hold a shape. Add flour as you work.
5. Place dough on a floured board and flour your hands. Form dough into rolls as wide as your finger and cut into 1-inch pieces. Press each piece gently against the inside of a fork or against a floured cheese grater to vary the texture and create a design.
6. Bring 4 quarts of water to a boil and add about 20 gnocchi at a time. When the gnocchi come to the surface, remove them from the pot with a slotted spoon and place in a serving dish. Moisten with a small amount of sauce. Repeat with remaining gnocchi and spoon sauce over them all.

Serves: 4

Orecchiette with Tomatoes and White Beans

Per serving: Fat: 2.9 grams Calories: 433

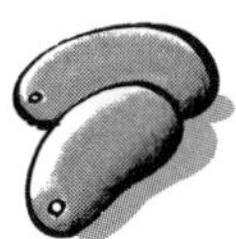

Olive oil cooking spray
3 garlic cloves, chopped
1 32-ounce can Italian plum tomatoes
1/4 cup dry red wine
Salt and freshly ground pepper to taste
1 cup cooked white beans (may be cannellini or Great Northern)
1/2 cup coarsely chopped basil
3/4 pound orecchiette pasta, cooked al dente
4 teaspoons grated Parmesan cheese

1. Coat a Dutch oven or large saucepan with cooking spray.
2. Add garlic and sauté, stirring, for 2 minutes. Be careful not to let garlic burn.
3. Add tomatoes, wine, and seasonings. Cook over medium heat for 20 minutes.
4. Add beans and basil. Lower heat and simmer for 15 minutes.
5. Transfer pasta to a serving bowl. Spoon bean sauce over pasta and toss to combine. Serve with Parmesan cheese.

Serves: 4

Fusilli with Red Bell Pepper Sauce I

PER SERVING: FAT: 2.7 GRAMS CALORIES: 491

Olive oil cooking spray
4 shallots, sliced
4 ROASTED RED BELL PEPPERS *(page 152)*
1 cup FAT-FREE CHICKEN BROTH *(page 52)*
1/2 cup dry red wine
1 tablespoon tomato paste
Salt and freshly ground pepper to taste
1 pound fusilli, cooked al dente
2 tablespoons chopped basil
4 teaspoons grated Parmesan cheese

1. Coat a large, nonstick skillet with cooking spray.
2. Add shallots and sauté, stirring frequently, for 5 minutes.
3. Cut 3 peppers into strips. Reserve remaining pepper. Place pepper strips, broth, wine, and tomato paste in a food processor. Puree.
4. Spoon puree into skillet and heat through. Season to taste with salt and pepper.
5. While sauce heats, cut remaining pepper into 1-inch squares.
6. Transfer fusilli to a serving bowl. Add sauce and toss to combine. Garnish with pepper squares and basil. Serve with Parmesan cheese.

Serves: 4

Fusilli with Red Bell Pepper Sauce II

PER SERVING: FAT: 4.0 GRAMS CALORIES: 499

Olive oil cooking spray
4 shallots, sliced
4 red bell peppers, roasted (page 152), cut into strips
1 cup FAT-FREE CHICKEN BROTH (page 52)
1/2 cup dry red wine
Salt and freshly ground pepper to taste
2 teaspoons whipped, light butter
1 pound fusilli, cooked al dente
2 tablespoons chopped basil
4 teaspoons grated Parmesan cheese

1. Coat a large, nonstick skillet with cooking spray.
2. Add shallots and sauté, stirring frequently, for 5 minutes.
3. In a food processor, combine the red peppers, broth, and wine. Puree. Depending on the size of your processor, you may have to do this in 2 or more steps.
4. Spoon puree into skillet and heat through. Season to taste with salt and pepper. When sauce is hot, stir in butter.
5. Transfer fusilli to a serving bowl. Add sauce and toss to combine. Garnish with basil. Serve with Parmesan cheese.

Serves: 4

Lasagna for a Dinner Party

PER SERVING: FAT: 1.6 GRAMS CALORIES: 414

2 pounds nonfat ricotta
Egg substitute equal to 2 eggs
1/4 cup chopped flat, or Italian, parsley
Salt and freshly ground pepper to taste
4 cups TOMATO-BASIL SAUCE *(page 157)*
1 pound curly-edged lasagna, cooked al dente
1/2 pound nonfat mozzarella cheese, shredded
1 tablespoon grated Parmesan cheese

Because you can prepare lasagna in advance, this dish is ideal for a party. When we were shooting *Prizzi's Honor,* I would put the lasagna together before going to work. When I got home after work, I would bake the lasagna while John Huston, Anjelica Huston, Jack, a few people from the crew, and I would play Trivial Pursuit for a few dollars.

1. Preheat oven to 400 degrees.
2. Combine ricotta, egg substitute, and parsley in a bowl. Mix until ingredients are thoroughly combined. Season with salt and pepper.
3. To assemble lasagna, spread a small amount of tomato-basil sauce on the bottom of a baking pan. Cover with a layer of lasagna. Top with ricotta cheese mixture. Add mozzarella. Continue layering until all ingredients are used. Final layers should be lasagna, sauce, and Parmesan cheese.
4. Cover dish with foil and bake for 30 minutes. Remove foil and bake for an additional 10 minutes.
5. Remove from oven and allow lasagna to rest for 15 minutes before slicing.

Serves: 8

Fettuccine Tossed with Mushrooms and Ricotta

PER SERVING: FAT: 4.4 GRAMS CALORIES: 429

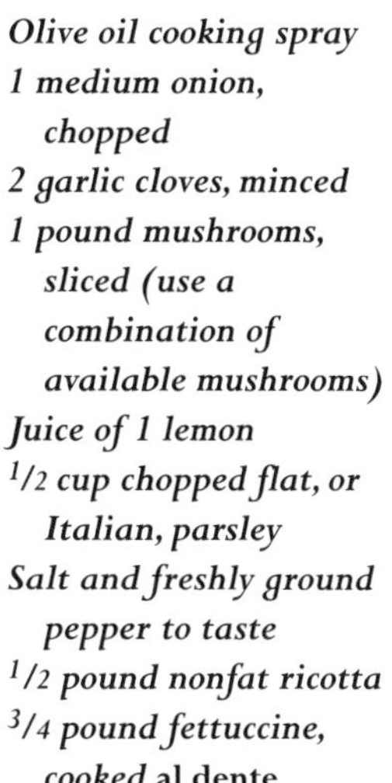

Olive oil cooking spray
1 medium onion, chopped
2 garlic cloves, minced
1 pound mushrooms, sliced (use a combination of available mushrooms)
Juice of 1 lemon
1/2 cup chopped flat, or Italian, parsley
Salt and freshly ground pepper to taste
1/2 pound nonfat ricotta
3/4 pound fettuccine, cooked al dente

1. Coat a large nonstick skillet with cooking spray, and heat.
2. Add onion and garlic and cook, stirring frequently, until onion is tender.
3. Add mushrooms and lemon. Stir to combine. Cover and cook over medium-low heat for 10 minutes.
4. Add parsley and season to taste with salt and pepper. Cover and cook an additional 10 minutes.
5. Stir in ricotta and cook over low heat, stirring, until ricotta has melted.
6. Spoon mushroom-ricotta combination over fettuccine and toss until combined. Serve immediately.

Serves: 4

Spaghetti and Turkey Meatballs

PER SERVING: FAT 5.2 GRAMS CALORIES: 782

2 slices stale bread, trimmed
1 cup skim milk
1 pound freshly ground breast of turkey
Egg substitute equal to 1 egg
3 tablespoons chopped flat, or Italian, parsley
1 garlic clove, minced
4 teaspoons grated Parmesan cheese
Salt and freshly ground pepper to taste
1/2 to 1 cup seasoned bread crumbs
Olive oil cooking spray
TOMATO-BASIL SAUCE (page 157)
1 pound spaghetti, cooked al dente

When I worked as a dialect coach on Prizzi's Honor, Anjelica Huston was having trouble with the Brooklyn accent necessary for her part. After years of private school in Ireland followed by finishing school, she couldn't get the intonation just right. I finally came up with the solution: I took Anjelica to my mother's house in Brooklyn one Sunday and they spent the day together. They had a wonderful time—first they went to church, and then they came back to the house to prepare Sunday dinner. My mother showed Anjelica how to make these meatballs—forever known in my mother's house as Anjelica's meatballs—and they went on to make about ten other courses. By the end of the day, Anjelica sounded more Brooklyn than anyone, and I don't know if it was the meatballs or my mother that did it. (Of course, my mother's meatballs were made with beef; this recipe calls for ground turkey, and the result is low fat, low calorie, and delicious.)

1. Preheat oven to 375 degrees.
2. Soak bread in milk until just softened. Squeeze out excess milk and place bread in a bowl.

3. Add ground turkey, egg substitute, parsley, garlic, Parmesan cheese, and seasonings. Mix until ingredients are thoroughly blended.
4. Add bread crumbs gradually, until mixture is firm enough to be shaped into meatballs; make them about 2 inches in diameter.
5. Coat a shallow, nonstick baking pan with cooking spray. Place meatballs in pan and bake, turning meatballs after 10 minutes, until lightly browned.
6. While meatballs brown, place sauce in a saucepan. Cover and bring to a simmer.
7. Add browned meatballs to sauce. Cover and cook over low heat for 30 minutes.
8. Place spaghetti (or other cooked pasta) in a serving bowl. Top with sauce and meatballs and toss gently before serving.

Serves: 4

Pasta and Fagioli

PER SERVING: FAT: 2.3 GRAMS CALORIES: 378

Olive oil cooking spray
1 medium onion, chopped
1/8 teaspoon crushed red pepper flakes (optional)
2 garlic cloves, chopped
1 medium carrot, chopped
2 celery stalks, chopped
4 plum tomatoes, peeled and chopped
1 cup FAT-FREE CHICKEN BROTH (page 52)
2 cups cooked cannellini beans
Salt and freshly ground pepper to taste
1/2 pound small pasta shells or elbows, cooked al dente
4 teaspoons grated Parmesan cheese

Everyone's heard of pasta-fagioli (or pasta e fagioli), the macaroni and bean combination that's served as a soup course, but I serve pasta-fagioli as a main course; and this dish is nicely filling even though it's comparatively low in calories and very low in fat. Traditionally, this dish is prepared with cannellini beans, but if you're looking to make an interesting change, prepare it with cooked chick peas instead.

1. Coat a Dutch oven or large saucepan with cooking spray.
2. Add onion and crushed red pepper and sauté, stirring, for 1 minute.
3. Add garlic, carrot, and celery and continue sautéing, stirring frequently, for 2 minutes.
4. Stir in tomatoes and sauté for an additional minute.
5. Add broth and bring to a simmer.
6. While liquid heats, puree half the beans. Add bean puree and remaining beans to liquid. Stir to combine. Season to taste with salt and pepper.
7. Cover and simmer over low heat for 5 minutes.
8. Add pasta to bean mixture and stir to combine.
9. Transfer to a serving bowl and serve with grated Parmesan cheese.

Serves: 4

Linguine Pescatore

Per serving: Fat: 3.5 grams Calories: 479

Olive oil cooking spray
1 small onion, diced
3 garlic cloves, minced
1/2 cup dry red wine
1 28-ounce can Italian crushed tomatoes
1/4 cup chopped basil
1 teaspoon oregano
1/4 teaspoon crushed red pepper flakes (optional)
Salt and freshly ground pepper to taste
1/2 pound medium shrimp, cleaned
8 tiny clams, scrubbed
8 mussels, scrubbed and debearded
4 scallops
1/2 pound cleaned and sliced squid (optional)
3/4 pound linguine, cooked al dente

1. Coat a large saucepan with spray.
2. Add onion and sauté for 2 minutes. Add garlic and sauté an additional minute, stirring occasionally.
3. Add wine and cook for an additional minute.
4. Add tomatoes, basil, oregano, and crushed red pepper flakes. Cover and bring to a simmer. Cook for 30 minutes. Season to taste.
5. Add shrimp, clams, mussels, scallops, and squid to sauce. Stir to combine and cook for 5 to 7 minutes.
6. Place pasta on a serving platter and pour seafood sauce over it. Remove and discard any clams or mussels that haven't opened. Toss pasta with sauce.

Serves: 4

Farfalle with Shrimp and Asparagus in Pesto

PER SERVING: FAT: 5.7 GRAMS CALORIES: 486

PESTO
1 cup packed basil leaves
1 teaspoon pine nuts
2 garlic cloves, cut in half
1/4 cup lemon juice
1/4 cup FAT-FREE CHICKEN BROTH (page 52)
1 teaspoon olive oil
1 tablespoon grated Parmesan cheese
Salt and freshly ground pepper to taste

SHRIMP
Olive oil cooking spray
1 pound large shrimp, trimmed and cut diagonally into 2-inch pieces
1 pound large shrimp, shelled and deveined
1/2 teaspoon crushed red pepper flakes (optional)
3/4 pound small farfalle (pasta bows), cooked al dente

PESTO

1. In a food processor, combine basil, pine nuts, garlic, lemon juice, broth, olive oil, and Parmesan cheese.
2. Process until finely pureed and season to taste with salt and pepper. Transfer pesto to a bowl and reserve.

SHRIMP AND ASPARAGUS

1. Coat a large nonstick skillet with spray. Add asparagus and cook until crisp-tender, about 5 minutes.
2. Add shrimp and red pepper flakes. Cook, stirring occasionally, until shrimp have turned pink.
3. Stir in pesto and heat through.
4. Place cooked farfalle on a large platter or in a bowl. Add shrimp-pesto combination and toss before serving.

Serves: 4

Shrimp with Tomato Sauce and Black Fettuccine

PER SERVING: FAT: 5.4 GRAMS CALORIES: 455

Olive oil cooking spray
1 small onion, finely chopped
2 garlic cloves, minced
1/2 cup dry white wine
1 28-ounce can Italian crushed tomatoes
1/2 teaspoon oregano
1/2 teaspoon crushed red pepper flakes (optional)
2 tablespoons chopped fresh basil
1 pound medium shrimp, cleaned
Salt and freshly ground pepper to taste
3/4 pound black fettuccine, cooked al dente

This is a dish that's as dramatic in looks as it is in flavor: the black fettuccine is topped with scarlet tomato sauce, which is covered with snowy shrimp. The combination of colors and flavors makes this one of my favorites.

1. Coat a large skillet with cooking spray.
2. Add onion and garlic and sauté for 5 minutes, stirring occasionally. Add wine.
3. Add tomatoes, oregano, crushed red pepper flakes, and basil. Cover and simmer for 20 minutes.
4. Add shrimp and simmer an additional 5 minutes. Season to taste with salt and pepper.
5. Place pasta on a serving platter. Top with sauce and then with shrimp.

Serves: 4

Spinach-Filled Manicotti with Tomato-Basil Sauce

PER SERVING (ONE SHELL): FAT: 1.5 GRAMS CALORIES: 98

SHELLS

1. Combine all ingredients, except for cooking spray, in a food processor. Process until thoroughly blended. Transfer to a container and refrigerate. Allow batter to rest for 15 to 20 minutes.
2. Lightly coat a nonstick stick crepe pan or omelette pan with cooking spray.
3. Heat pan and pour or spoon a small amount of batter into pan. Tilt pan so that batter covers bottom of pan. Brown lightly. Turn and brown second side.
4. Transfer shell to a plate and repeat with remaining batter.

Yield: About 8 shells

FILLING

1. Preheat oven to 375 degrees.
2. Combine all ingredients, except for sauce, in a bowl. Mix thoroughly.
3. Spread 2 tablespoons of filling on each shell and roll.
4. Spread 1/2 cup of tomato-basil sauce in a baking dish. Place filled shells in dish and spoon 1/2 cup over them.
5. Bake until heated through, about 15 to 20 minutes. Serve with remaining sauce.

Serves: 8 as an appetizer, 4 as a main dish

SHELLS

1/2 cup all-purpose flour
Egg substitute equivalent to 1 egg
1/2 cup water
Pinch of salt
Vegetable oil cooking spray

FILLING

1/2 pound nonfat ricotta cheese
1 tablespoon grated Parmesan cheese
1/4 cup shredded nonfat mozzarella cheese
1/2 pound spinach, blanched, drained, and chopped (1/2 package of frozen chopped spinach, thawed, may be substituted)
Salt and freshly ground pepper to taste
1 1/2 cups TOMATO-BASIL SAUCE (page 157)

Wild Mushroom Ravioli With Vegetable Sauce

PER SERVING: FAT 7.75 GRAMS CALORIES: 358

Olive oil cooking spray
2 garlic cloves, sliced
1 small zucchini, finely chopped
1 small yellow squash, finely chopped
1 small carrot, finely chopped
1 small red onion, finely chopped
2 plum tomatoes, finely chopped
2 small Italian eggplant (about 1/2 pound), peeled and finely chopped
2 tablespoons chopped basil
1/2 cup dry white wine
1 1/2 cups vegetable broth
Salt and freshly ground pepper to taste
1/8 teaspoon crushed red pepper flakes (optional)
2 teaspoons light whipped butter
1 pound wild mushroom ravioli, cooked al dente*
2 teaspoons grated Parmesan cheese

1. Coat a large, nonstick skillet with cooking spray.
2. Add garlic and sauté, stirring, for 1 minute.
3. Add all vegetables, basil, wine, broth, salt, pepper, and red pepper flakes.
4. Bring to a boil. Lower heat and simmer, uncovered, for 5 minutes, or until vegetables are just tender.
5. Whisk in butter and cook until sauce has thickened slightly.
6. Place ravioli in a serving bowl. Top with sauce and toss gently. Serve with Parmesan cheese.

Serves: 4

*Spinach ravioli may be substituted.

Classic Baked Ziti

PER SERVING: FAT: 2.5 GRAMS CALORIES: 532

Olive oil cooking spray
1 small onion, diced
2 garlic cloves, minced
1 small carrot, grated
1 28-ounce can Italian crushed tomatoes
1 cup chopped basil
Salt and freshly ground pepper to taste
3/4 pound ziti, cooked al dente
1/4 pound nonfat mozzarella cheese, shredded
1 pound fat-free ricotta
2 teaspoons grated Parmesan cheese

I make this dish when I'm at Jack's house and we're planning to watch a Lakers basketball game, football, the fights, or some other sporting event. I never know how many people are going to come by to watch the game, so I make a big pan of ziti. Sometimes there are even leftovers. When that happens, I transfer whatever is left to a foil pan, cover the pan, and freeze the ziti. This really comes in handy when unexpected people come by. I just take the ziti out of the freezer, defrost, heat, and dress it up with some nonfat ricotta and mozzarella. Believe me, this does not taste like a sad leftover. If you're ever left with a large, uneaten portion of a pasta dish, don't throw it out. Just do what I do with the ziti.

Jack has a full-time live-in chef at his Hollywood house—and it isn't me. I do cook for Jack when he's on location and when I stay with him at his home, but I can't be there all the time, so I've trained his chef to follow my recipes. In addition, during the time I stay with Jack, I prepare gallons of TOMATO-BASIL SAUCE (page 157) and quarts of PASTA AND FAGIOLI (page 88), as well as ESCAROLE SOUP (page 53). All these dishes can be frozen successfully. I just portion them into different-sized containers so that even when I'm not around Jack can enjoy his favorites.

It's great cooking at Jack's house—I don't have to clean up! My advice: When you're whomping up a big meal, get your spouse or significant other—whatever—to do the cleaning up. It's only fair.

1. Preheat oven to 350 degrees.
2. Coat a large nonstick skillet with cooking spray.
3. Add onion, garlic, and carrot. Sauté for 1 minute, stirring.
4. Add tomatoes, basil, and seasonings. Cover and cook over medium heat for 30 minutes.
5. Add ziti to sauce and toss.
6. Stir in mozzarella and ricotta and heat through.
7. Transfer to a serving bowl and serve with Parmesan cheese.

Serves: 4

PASTA WITH LENTILS

Here's another bean and pasta dish that's just a little different. Instead of cannellini beans, I use lentils. Follow the recipe for PASTA AND FAGIOLI (page 88), but when you get to step 6, don't puree the lentils. Other than that, the recipe stays the same.

Chapter Six

POULTRY

POULTRY IS THE MEAT lowest in fat and calories—especially when you cook it the way I do, without the skin. Most of the fat and calories lurk in the skin, so get rid of it!

Flavor poultry with spices, glaze, fruits, vegetables, and herbs. The nice thing about poultry is that its mild character allows many different flavor combinations, and it can be roasted, grilled, broiled, stewed, sautéed, and stir-fried.

I like to prepare a dinner that starts out with a vegetable appetizer—eggplant spread (page 43), maybe, or bean dip (page 42). I then go to a pasta dish, and follow with chicken. When I serve pasta as a second course, I usually cut the recipe in half, and then I go ahead with chicken as the main course. Lots of food, but very little fat. Sometimes I use turkey—now that's really low in fat—and as everyone knows by now, turkey isn't just for Thanksgiving anymore.

Glazed Apricot Chicken

PER SERVING: FAT: 2.5 GRAMS CALORIES: 259

Vegetable oil cooking spray
2 tablespoons lemon juice
2 garlic cloves, finely chopped
2 skinless chicken breasts, split, bone in (about 2 pounds)
Salt and freshly ground pepper to taste
8 dried apricots
3/4 cup orange juice
1 teaspoon light brown sugar
1 teaspoon cider vinegar
1 tablespoon shredded ginger
1 teaspoon Dijon mustard

1. Preheat oven to 375 degrees.
2. Lightly coat a baking pan with vegetable oil cooking spray.
3. Combine lemon juice and garlic and spoon all over chicken. Season with salt and pepper.
4. Bake chicken for 20 minutes.
5. While chicken bakes, combine apricots and orange juice in a saucepan and bring liquid to a simmer. Cook for about 10 minutes, or until apricots are tender.
6. Add all remaining ingredients to apricots and mix to combine.
7. Transfer apricot mixture to a food processor and puree.
8. Spoon half of apricot sauce over chicken and bake for 10 minutes.
9. Turn chicken and spoon remainder of apricot sauce over chicken.
10. Bake an additional 10 minutes.

Serves: 4

Chicken with Bell Peppers

PER SERVING: FAT: 3.7 GRAMS CALORIES: 307

2 skinless chicken breasts, split, bone in (about 2 pounds)
Salt and freshly ground pepper to taste
Vegetable oil cooking spray
1 red bell pepper, sliced
1 green bell pepper, sliced
1 yellow or orange bell pepper, sliced
3 garlic cloves, thinly sliced
1 medium onion, thinly sliced
1 pound mushrooms, thinly sliced
1 32-ounce can plum tomatoes, with liquid
1/2 cup dry white wine
1 teaspoon oregano
1/4 cup chopped basil leaves

1. Season chicken with salt and pepper.
2. Coat a large, nonstick skillet with vegetable oil cooking spray.
3. Add chicken to skillet and brown lightly on all sides, turning frequently. Remove chicken and reserve.
4. Add bell peppers, garlic, onion, and mushrooms. Sauté for 5 minutes. Add tomatoes with half their liquid, wine, oregano, and basil to skillet. Reserve remainder of liquid from tomatoes.
5. Return chicken to skillet and cook until chicken is cooked through, about 30 minutes. Sauce should be thick, not dry or soupy. If necessary, add reserved tomato juice to skillet, 2 tablespoons at a time.
6. Transfer chicken to a platter and serve.

Serves: 4

Party Time Chili

PER SERVING: FAT: 1.4 GRAMS CALORIES: 219

Vegetable oil cooking spray
2 large red onions, finely chopped
2 green bell peppers, finely chopped
2 garlic cloves, minced
2 pounds breast of turkey, coarsely chopped (Do not use ground turkey.)
1 28-ounce can crushed tomatoes
1 2-ounce can tomato paste
1 jalapeño chili pepper, cored, seeded, and minced (or to taste)
1 cup beer
1/2 teaspoon cumin
2 teaspoons chili powder (or to taste)
2 cups cooked kidney or pinto beans
Salt to taste

1. Coat a heavy saucepan with cooking spray. Heat and add onions, bell peppers, and garlic. Sauté, stirring, until onions are translucent.
2. Add turkey to saucepan, a little at a time, stirring, until turkey is lightly browned.
3. Add all remaining ingredients, except for beans and salt. Bring to a boil. Lower heat to a simmer and cook, covered, for about 1 hour, stirring occasionally.
4. Add beans to saucepan. Stir and cook, covered, an additional 30 minutes. Correct seasoning. May be served with chopped onion, shredded nonfat cheese, and nonfat sour cream.

Serves: 8 to 10

Quick Curried Chicken

PER SERVING: FAT: 2.2 GRAMS CALORIES: 165

Vegetable oil cooking spray
1 small onion, chopped
1 clove garlic, chopped
1 skinless, boneless breast of chicken (about 1 pound), cut into strips
1 teaspoon curry powder
1/2 cup nonfat plain yogurt
4 scallions, diced
1 teaspoon sesame seeds

1. Coat a large, nonstick skillet with vegetable oil cooking spray.
2. Add onion and garlic and sauté, stirring, for 1 minute.
3. Add chicken and sauté, stirring occasionally, until chicken is cooked.
4. In a small bowl combine curry powder and yogurt. Mix to combine and add to skillet.
5. Continue cooking chicken in curry-yogurt sauce until all ingredients are heated through.
6. Transfer curried chicken to a serving platter or 4 plates. Garnish with scallions and sesame seeds and serve with rice, if you wish.

Serves: 4

Hunter's-Style Chicken

PER SERVING: FAT: 3.1 GRAMS CALORIES: 257

2 skinless chicken breasts, split, bone in (about 2 pounds)
All-purpose flour for coating chicken
Olive oil cooking spray
3 garlic cloves, sliced
1 pound mushrooms, thinly sliced
2 tablespoons red wine vinegar
1 cup dry white wine
1 2-ounce can tomato paste
1 cup water
2 teaspoons oregano
1/2 teaspoon crushed red pepper flakes (optional)
Salt and freshly ground pepper to taste

1. Coat chicken lightly with flour, shaking off excess.
2. Coat a large, nonstick skillet with cooking spray.
3. Heat skillet and add chicken. Cook, turning, until lightly browned.
4. Add garlic and mushrooms and cook for 1 minute.
5. Add remaining ingredients. Stir to combine.
6. Cover skillet and cook for 45 to 50 minutes, allowing flavors to blend. If sauce is too thick, add water, 1 or 2 tablespoons at a time. Serve with pasta, rice, or polenta.

Serves: 4

Grilled Chicken with Assorted Greens

PER SERVING: FAT: 2.6 GRAMS CALORIES: 211

2 cups chopped assorted lettuce
3 tablespoons CITRUS VINAIGRETTE *(page 156)*
1 1/2 pounds chicken cutlets
1/2 small onion, diced
2 garlic cloves, minced
1/2 cup FAT-FREE CHICKEN BROTH *(page 52)*
2 tablespoons chopped dill
1/4 cup lemon juice
Salt and freshly ground pepper to taste
Olive oil cooking spray

1. Place lettuce in a bowl and toss with citrus vinaigrette. Refrigerate until ready to serve.
2. Place chicken cutlets in a shallow pan. Combine all remaining ingredients, except for cooking spray, in a bowl. Mix thoroughly and pour over chicken.
3. Refrigerate chicken and turn in marinade every 15 minutes. Allow chicken to marinate for at least 1 hour.
4. Chicken may be cooked on an outdoor barbecue or gas grill. It may also be cooked on a stovetop grill. If cooking indoors, coat grill or a nonstick skillet with cooking spray. Heat and add chicken. Cook over medium-high heat, turning, until chicken is lightly browned on both sides and cooked through, about 5 minutes.
5. To serve, place assorted greens on 4 dinner plates and top with chicken. Chicken may also be served on a bun with sliced tomatoes and with greens on the side.

Serves: 4

Lemon 'n' Lime Chicken

PER SERVING: FAT: 6.5 GRAMS CALORIES: 175

1 3- to $3^1/2$-pound chicken
3 garlic cloves
Salt and freshly ground pepper to taste
2 lemons
2 limes
1 tablespoon chopped fresh rosemary, or 1 teaspoon dry rosemary
1 cup water

I prepared this dish a lot when we were shooting <u>Wolf</u> in 1993, and whenever Michelle Pfeiffer learned that it was on the menu, she'd appear at the camper and join us for dinner. Will a movie star appear at your kitchen door when you make this dish? No guarantee, but you never know.

1. Preheat oven to 500 degrees.
2. Wash chicken inside and out and dry thoroughly with paper towels. (Chicken must be dry or it won't brown.)
3. Cut 1 garlic clove in half, and rub garlic over chicken, both inside and out. Place remaining 2 cloves in cavity.
4. Season chicken with salt and pepper.
5. Roll 1 lemon and 1 lime on a hard surface. This helps release the juices. Prick lemon and lime in 5 or 6 places and place in cavity of chicken. Add rosemary and remaining garlic.
6. Place chicken in a shallow, nonstick pan and brown in oven for 15 minutes.
7. Remove chicken from oven and reduce heat to 350 degrees.
8. Squeeze juice from remaining lemon and lime and add to chicken. Stir in water.
9. Cover pan with a foil tent and return chicken to oven. Roast for an additional 45 minutes, or until chicken is cooked through.
10. Remove skin before carving and serve chicken with pan juices.

Serves: 6

Chicken 'n' Rice

Per serving: Fat: 3.1 grams Calories: 422

Olive oil cooking spray
2 skinless and boneless chicken breasts (about 1 1/2 pounds)
1 garlic clove, minced
1 medium carrot, diced
1/2 pound mushrooms, thinly sliced
4 plum tomatoes, diced
1 cup rice
1/2 cup dry white wine
1 1/2 cups FAT-FREE CHICKEN BROTH (page 52)
Salt and freshly ground pepper to taste
2 tablespoons minced flat, or Italian, parsley

1. Coat a large skillet with cooking spray. Heat skillet.
2. Add chicken and brown lightly, turning once or twice. Remove chicken from skillet and reserve.
3. Add garlic, carrot, and mushrooms to skillet. Cook, stirring occasionally, for 3 minutes.
4. Add tomatoes and rice to skillet and sauté until rice becomes opaque.
5. Return chicken to skillet and add wine and half of the broth.
6. Cover skillet and cook over medium heat until liquid is absorbed.
7. Add remainder of broth and continue cooking until liquid is absorbed, by which time rice should be tender. If rice is not completely tender, add 1 or 2 tablespoons of water and continue cooking.
8. Season to taste with salt and pepper and stir in parsley.
9. Transfer to a platter and serve.

Serves: 4

Chicken with Marsala

Per serving: Fat: 1.7 grams Calories: 204

1/4 cup all-purpose flour
1/4 teaspoon freshly ground pepper
Salt to taste
1/2 cup marsala wine
1/4 cup FAT-FREE CHICKEN BROTH *(page 52)*
1 pound chicken cutlets, pounded thin
Olive oil cooking spray
1 garlic clove, minced

1. Combine flour, pepper, and salt in a bowl. Mix thoroughly. Reserve.
2. In another bowl, combine wine, broth, and 1 teaspoon of the seasoned flour. Mix until blended. Reserve.
3. Lightly coat chicken cutlets with remaining seasoned flour, shaking off excess.
4. Coat a large nonstick skillet with olive oil cooking spray. Heat skillet and add cutlets. Cook cutlets until lightly browned on both sides, about 4 minutes per side.
5. Remove chicken from skillet and keep warm.
6. Add garlic to skillet and sauté, stirring over low heat, being careful not to let garlic brown.
7. Add wine mixture to skillet and cook, stirring, for 1 minute.
8. Return chicken to skillet and cook, turning, until chicken is well-coated with sauce and all ingredients are heated through.
9. Transfer chicken to a serving platter and spoon remaining sauce over chicken. Serve with rice.

Serves: 4

Chicken in Orange-Mustard Sauce

PER SERVING: FAT: 2.5 GRAMS CALORIES: 272

Olive oil cooking spray
2 boneless, skinless chicken breasts, split (about $1^{1}/_{2}$ pounds)
Salt and freshly ground pepper to taste
3 shallots, thinly sliced
2 teaspoons cornstarch
1 cup orange juice
5 teaspoons Dijon mustard
1 cup mandarin orange sections
1 tablespoon chopped flat, or Italian, parsley

1. Preheat oven to 400 degrees.
2. Coat a nonstick skillet with cooking spray.
3. Add chicken and brown lightly on both sides.
4. Coat a nonstick baking pan with cooking spray and transfer chicken to pan. Season to taste with salt and pepper.
5. Bake chicken for about 15 minutes, or until done.
6. While chicken bakes, coat skillet again with cooking spray. Add shallots and sauté until translucent.
7. Combine cornstarch and juice in a bowl and mix well. Add mixture to skillet gradually. Stir in mustard and bring sauce to a boil. Reduce heat to a simmer and cook sauce until it thickens.
8. Stir in orange sections.
9. Place chicken on a platter and top with sauce. Garnish with parsley. May be served with rice.

Serves: 4

Chapter Seven

FISH AND SHELLFISH

I PREPARE A LOT OF FISH and shellfish. There's no big secret to fine fish cooking. Fish has to be fresh, really fresh—that's the rule. And while you've heard that before, not everyone pays attention to the rule. I know you've read in many other books about clear-eyed, firm-fleshed, non-smelly fish. That's the way it has to be, and there's no room for compromise.

Now it's up to you to find a local fish store that you can really trust.

Once you've purchased fine, fresh fish or shellfish—and at today's prices it had better be good—what do you do next? Prepare it as simply as possible. Fresh fish doesn't need cream or thick, floury sauces to disguise the taste.

My recipes call for broths, simple sauces, and the addition of vegetables—as I've said, I try to include vegetables whenever I can. And for more ways to prepare seafood, look at the chapter on pasta—lots of good ideas there, too.

Fish Chowder for Company

Per serving: Fat: 2.0 grams Calories: 304

Olive oil cooking spray
1 medium onion, chopped
2 carrots, sliced
5 leeks, white part only, chopped
2 large green bell peppers, chopped
8 plum tomatoes, chopped
4 medium potatoes, cubed
1/2 cup clam juice
1 cup dry white wine
1 teaspoon thyme
2 tablespoons chopped flat, or Italian, parsley
1 teaspoon crushed red pepper flakes, or to taste
1 bay leaf
Salt to taste
1 pound cod (or other white-meat fish), cubed
1 pound sea scallops
1/2 pound shrimp, cleaned
1 12-ounce can evaporated skim milk

1. Coat a large soup pot or Dutch oven with cooking spray. Add onion, carrots, leeks, and green bell peppers. Sauté for 5 minutes, stirring occasionally.
2. Add tomatoes, potatoes, clam juice, wine, thyme, parsley, red pepper flakes, bay leaf, and salt.
3. Bring to a boil. Lower heat to a simmer and cover. Cook for 15 minutes.
4. Add fish, scallops, and shrimp. Cook for 10 minutes. Remove and discard bay leaf.
5. Add milk, stir to combine, and just heat through. Serve in bowls.

Serves: 8

Fillet of Salmon with Ginger-Basil Sauce

PER SERVING: FAT: 10.9 GRAMS CALORIES: 284

4 6-ounce salmon fillets
1 cup dry white wine
1/2 cup seasoned rice wine vinegar
1 shallot, sliced
2 garlic cloves, chopped
2 tablespoons chopped ginger
1 tablespoon light soy sauce
1 tablespoon nonfat sour cream
1/2 cup chopped basil

1. Place salmon fillets in a fish poacher or a skillet large enough to hold fish side by side.
2. Add wine and cover. Poach fish in liquid for 10 minutes.
3. Remove fish using a slotted spoon or spatula, and reserve.
4. In a saucepan combine vinegar, shallot, garlic, and ginger. Bring to a boil. Lower heat and allow sauce to simmer until reduced by half.
5. Strain sauce and discard solids. Return liquid to saucepan and add soy sauce and sour cream. Stir and transfer to a sauce boat or bowl. Serve sauce with salmon and garnish with basil.

Serves: 4

Fillet of Salmon with Vegetables

Per serving: Fat: 11.4 grams Calories: 454

Vegetable oil cooking spray
2 medium onions, cut into rings
4 medium potatoes, thinly sliced
2 carrots, thinly sliced
4 salmon fillets (about 6 ounces each)
1 tablespoon chopped dill
Salt and freshly ground pepper to taste
1 cup FAT-FREE CHICKEN BROTH (page 52)
1/2 cup dry white wine

1. Coat a nonstick skillet with cooking spray.
2. Add onions and potatoes and sauté for 3 to 4 minutes, stirring occasionally.
3. Add carrots and sauté an additional 2 minutes.
4. Place salmon in skillet in one layer. Add dill and season to taste with salt and pepper.
5. Add broth and wine to skillet. Liquid should cover fish; add more broth or water if necessary.
6. Bring liquid to a boil. Reduce heat to a simmer. Cover and cook until fish is cooked through. Salmon should be opaque in the center.
7. Place a salmon fillet on a dinner plate and spoon vegetables and sauce over fish. Repeat with remaining ingredients.

Serves: 4

Scallops with Cilantro and Lime

PER SERVING: FAT: 1.2 GRAMS CALORIES: 125

Olive oil cooking spray
2 garlic cloves, pressed
1 pound sea scallops, cut in half horizontally
2 scallions, minced
1/2 teaspoon hot pepper sauce (or to taste)
1/4 cup dry white wine
1/4 cup lime juice
Salt and freshly ground pepper to taste
2 tablespoons minced cilantro
1 lime, thinly sliced

1. Coat a large nonstick skillet with cooking spray.
2. Add garlic and cook, stirring, for 30 seconds.
3. Add scallops, scallions, and hot pepper sauce and sauté, stirring, over medium-high heat for 2 minutes.
4. Add wine and lime juice and continue sautéing and stirring for 3 minutes, or until scallops are just cooked. Do not overcook or scallops will toughen.
5. Transfer scallops to a platter. Season with salt and pepper and garnish with cilantro and lime slices before serving. If you wish, serve with LAYERED POTATOES (page 143).

Serves: 4

Baked Fillet of Scrod

PER SERVING: FAT: 2.1 GRAMS CALORIES: 206

Vegetable oil cooking spray
1 medium onion, chopped
2 garlic cloves, minced
1/4 pound mushrooms, sliced
1 yellow or red bell pepper, sliced
1 tablespoon capers, rinsed and drained
4 plum tomatoes, chopped
4 black or green pitted olives, sliced
1 tablespoon chopped basil
1/2 teaspoon oregano
Salt and freshly ground pepper to taste
1/2 cup dry white wine
4 6-ounce fillets of scrod or other thick, white-meat fish

1. Preheat oven to 400 degrees.
2. Coat a large, nonstick skillet with cooking spray.
3. Add onion and garlic and sauté, stirring, for 1 minute.
4. Add mushrooms and pepper and continue sautéing, stirring occasionally, for about 3 minutes.
5. Stir in capers, tomatoes, olives, basil, oregano, salt, and pepper.
6. Add wine and bring to a boil. Lower heat and cook, stirring, until sauce just thickens.
7. Place fish fillets in one layer in a baking dish.
8. Spoon sauce over fish and bake for 20 minutes, or until fish is just cooked through. Serve with rice, if you wish.

   Serves: 4

Seafood Papillote

Per serving: Fat: 2.3 grams Calories: 187

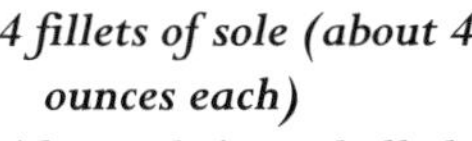

4 fillets of sole (about 4 ounces each)
4 large shrimp, shelled and deveined
4 sea scallops
4 mussels, scrubbed and debearded
4 littleneck clams
1 cup TOMATO-BASIL SAUCE *(page 157)*
1/4 cup dry white wine
1/4 cup chopped basil
4 pieces aluminum foil

1. Preheat oven to 400 degrees.
2. On each piece of aluminum foil place 1 fillet of sole, 1 shrimp, 1 scallop, 1 mussel, 1 clam, 4 tablespoons of sauce, 1 tablespoon of wine, and 1 tablespoon of basil.
3. Wrap foil around ingredients, folding twice on top and twice at the ends, and place foil packets in a shallow baking dish.
4. Bake seafood for 20 minutes. Foil will puff.
5. Place 1 packet on each dinner plate, and carefully cut an X in foil, allowing steam to escape. Serve immediately.

Serves: 4

One-Dish Dinner: Shrimp in Broth

PER SERVING: FAT: 2.2 GRAMS CALORIES: 165

1 pound large shrimp
1 carrot, chopped
1 celery stalk, chopped
3 garlic cloves, chopped
1 small onion
1 large fennel bulb, chopped
4 plum tomatoes, chopped
2 tablespoons flat, or Italian, parsley, chopped
Salt and freshly ground pepper to taste
8 cups water
1 pound spinach, washed and trimmed
1/2 pound Chinese vermicelli or angel-hair pasta, cooked al dente *(optional)*

1. Shell and devein shrimp. Place shrimp in bowl and refrigerate. Place shrimp shells in a large soup pot.
2. Add all remaining ingredients, except for spinach, shrimp, and pasta, to pot.
3. Cover pot and bring liquid to a boil. Reduce to a simmer and cook for 1 hour.
4. Strain liquid and discard solids. Return liquid to a simmer and add spinach and shrimp. Cook for 3 to 4 minutes.
5. To serve, ladle soup with shrimp into 4 bowls. If using pasta, place pasta in bowls first and top with soup and shrimp.

Serves: 4

Fillet of Red Snapper in Ginger-Orange Sauce

PER SERVING: FAT: 2.3 GRAMS CALORIES: 229

1 tablespoon minced ginger
1/2 cup orange juice
1/4 cup dry white wine
1 navel orange, peeled and chopped
2 teaspoons cornstarch
1/4 cup water
2 tablespoons chopped flat, or Italian, parsley
1 1/2 cups FAT-FREE CHICKEN BROTH (page 52)
4 6-ounce fillets of red snapper (striped bass or other white-meat fish may be used)
Salt and freshly ground pepper to taste

1. In a saucepan combine ginger, orange juice, and white wine. Bring to a simmer and stir in orange.
2. In a small bowl combine cornstarch and water and mix until blended. Add cornstarch mixture to ginger-orange juice combination and simmer until sauce thickens. Stir in parsley and keep warm.
3. Heat broth in a large skillet. Add fish fillets in one layer. Cover and poach gently for about 10 minutes, or until fish is just cooked through.
4. Using a slotted spatula, remove fish from broth and place on 4 dinner plates. Season to taste with salt and pepper.
5. Spoon ginger-orange sauce over fish and serve.

Serves: 4

Grilled Swordfish with Mixed Bean Salsa

Per serving: Fat: 8.2 grams Calories: 384

1 cup cooked cannellini beans
1 cup cooked kidney beans
1 cup cooked black beans
2 garlic cloves, chopped
1 medium onion, chopped
1 tablespoon cilantro, chopped
1 tablespoon flat, or Italian, parsley, chopped
1 teaspoon olive oil
2 tablespoons balsamic vinegar
Salt and freshly ground pepper to taste
Olive oil cooking spray
4 6-ounce swordfish steaks

The bean salsa served with the swordfish can be prepared with a variety of beans. If you don't want to prepare two or three kinds of beans, a one-bean salsa will also work.

1. In a large bowl, combine beans, garlic, onion, cilantro, parsley, oil, vinegar, and seasonings. Mix thoroughly.
2. Refrigerate bean salsa for at least 1 hour before serving.
3. Preheat oven to broil. (Fish may also be grilled.)
4. Spray a broiling pan with cooking spray.
5. Place fish on broiling pan and spray lightly with cooking spray.
6. Broil fish for 5 minutes. Turn and broil second side for an additional 5 minutes or until fish is cooked to taste.
7. To serve, spoon bean salsa into the center of 4 dinner plates. Place swordfish steak on top of beans and serve.

Serves: 4

Monkfish in Sesame Seed Crust with Red Pepper Sauce

PER SERVING: FAT: 6.2 GRAMS CALORIES: 245

2 tablespoons sesame seeds
3/4 cup plain bread crumbs
Salt and white pepper to taste
4 6-ounce monkfish fillets
2 egg whites, lightly beaten
Olive oil cooking spray
RED BELL PEPPER SAUCE III (page 153)

1. Preheat oven to 375 degrees.
2. In a large bowl, mix sesame seeds, bread crumbs, and seasonings.
3. Dip fish into egg whites and coat with crumb mixture. Press crumbs into fish with fingertips.
4. Coat a nonstick skillet with cooking spray and sear fish in skillet on both sides. Be careful not to let crumb crust blacken and burn.
5. Transfer fish to a nonstick baking pan and lightly spray top of fish with cooking spray.
6. Bake fish until cooked to taste. Fish is best if not overcooked.
7. Spread red bell pepper sauce on 4 dinner plates and top with fish.

Serves: 4

Chapter Eight

MEAT

I THINK THAT HEALTHY EATING should include something from every food group, and the low-fat dishes I cook do include meat. I'm not saying you can eat pounds of well-marbled beef steak and lose weight, but I do believe you can enjoy meat in small quantities and keep your weight down.

Here are my low-fat, low-calorie recipes for beef, pork, veal, and lamb, and you'll be pleased to know that pork tenderloin contains no more fat than skinless chicken.

If you have a meal higher in fat due to meat, make up for it during the next few days by choosing carefully from our low-fat recipes.

Kathleen Turner's Sicilian Steak Giardiniera

PER SERVING: FAT: 4.1 GRAMS CALORIES: 168

Olive oil cooking spray
1 medium onion, cut into thin rings
1 pound lean, boneless top round, cut across the grain into strips
1 cup pickled mixed vegetables, drained, pickling mixture reserved
MARYLOU'S LOW-FAT HOME FRIES (page 141)

Kathleen Turner has a brownstone in Greenwich Village near our restaurant, and she's also my neighbor in the Hamptons. We often combine forces and cook together when one of us is giving a dinner party. I devised this recipe for her after I helped her drop some pounds and she called me a "Sicilian diet guru"—what a combination! I'm not a guru, and I don't do diets.

Anyway, I created this recipe when we were in the mood for steak. This dish combines quickly sautéed lean beef with pickled vegetables. The vegetables add so much flavor you won't notice that you're not eating a huge porterhouse.

1. Coat a large skillet with cooking spray.
2. Add onion rings and sauté over medium-high heat until lightly browned. Remove onion rings and reserve.
3. Increase heat and add meat strips. Cook, stirring constantly, until meat has just lost its raw, red color. Remove from skillet and add to onion rings.
4. Add pickled vegetables to skillet and heat through.
5. Return onion rings and beef to skillet. Add 2 tablespoons of pickling liquid. Cook over high heat, stirring, until beef is heated through. Transfer to a platter and serve with Marylou's home fries.

Serves: 4

Roast Lamb Shanks with Orzo

PER SERVING: FAT: 5.3 GRAMS CALORIES: 437

4 small lamb shanks, trimmed of visible fat
Olive oil cooking spray
2 large onions, sliced
Salt and freshly ground pepper to taste
4 garlic cloves, minced
1 32-ounce can Italian plum tomatoes
1 cup dry white wine
2 cups fat-free beef broth
1 cup orzo

1. Preheat oven to 400 degrees.
2. Place lamb shanks in a shallow pan and roast, turning, until meat has browned on all sides. Discard fat that has rendered from meat.
3. While lamb roasts, coat an ovenproof Dutch oven with spray.
4. Add onions and sauté until lightly browned.
5. Remove roasting pan from oven and reduce heat to 375 degrees. Using a slotted spatula remove lamb from pan and place in Dutch oven.
6. Season lamb with salt and pepper and add garlic.
7. Drain tomatoes, reserving the juice, and add tomatoes, wine, and broth to lamb. Stir until liquids are combined.
8. Cover Dutch oven and place in oven. Roast for about 45 minutes, or until lamb is almost tender.
9. Stir in orzo and continue roasting until lamb and orzo are tender, about 15 minutes. If additional liquid is needed, add reserved tomato juice 1 to 2 tablespoons at a time.
10. Serve immediately or remove to top of stove and heat before serving.

Serves: 4

Braised Veal Shanks

PER SERVING: FAT: 4.4 GRAMS CALORIES: 225

Olive oil cooking spray
4 pieces veal shank, each about 2 inches long
2 tablespoons all-purpose flour
Salt and freshly ground pepper to taste
1 medium onion, chopped
1 medium carrot, finely chopped
1 celery stalk, thinly sliced
1 garlic clove, chopped
1 cup fat-free beef broth
1 cup dry white wine
1 28-ounce can crushed tomatoes
1/2 teaspoon rosemary
1 bay leaf
2 tablespoons chopped flat, or Italian, parsley
1 tablespoon grated lemon peel

1. Lightly coat a Dutch oven with cooking spray and heat.
2. Coat each veal shank with flour, shake off excess, and season to taste with salt and pepper.
3. Brown veal lightly on all sides. Remove from Dutch oven and reserve.
4. Add onion, carrot, and celery to pot and sauté for 1 minute, stirring. Add garlic and sauté an additional minute.
5. Add broth, wine, tomatoes, rosemary, and bay leaf. Stir to combine.
6. Return veal to pot. Cover and cook over low heat for 45 minutes, or until veal is almost fork-tender.
7. Stir in parsley and lemon peel. Cover and cook an additional 15 minutes or until veal is completely tender. Remove and discard bay leaf. Serve with rice or pasta.

Serves: 4

Pork Medallions with Spinach and Ricotta

Per serving: Fat: 6.6 grams Calories: 191

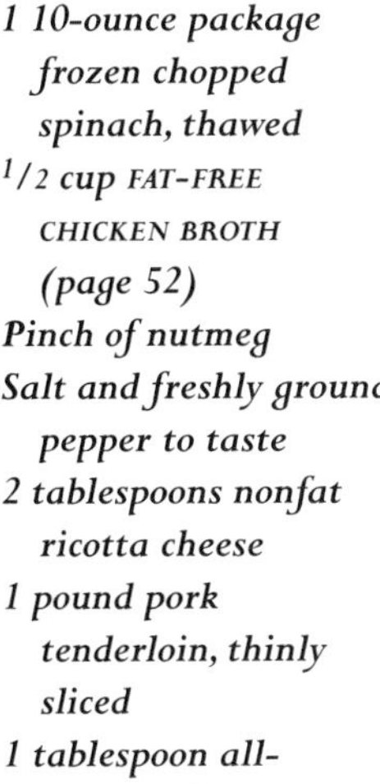

1 10-ounce package frozen chopped spinach, thawed
1/2 cup FAT-FREE CHICKEN BROTH *(page 52)*
Pinch of nutmeg
Salt and freshly ground pepper to taste
2 tablespoons nonfat ricotta cheese
1 pound pork tenderloin, thinly sliced
1 tablespoon all-purpose flour
Olive oil cooking spray

1. Combine spinach, broth, and nutmeg in a saucepan. Cover and cook over low heat for 5 minutes.
2. Season spinach with salt and pepper and stir in ricotta.
3 Transfer spinach mixture to a food processor and puree.
4. Return spinach mixture to saucepan and reserve.
5. Dust pork lightly with flour.
6. Spray a nonstick skillet with cooking spray and heat skillet.
7. Add pork to skillet and sauté, turning, until lightly browned and cooked through.
8. While pork cooks, gently heat spinach sauce.
9. Spoon sauce onto a serving platter and top with pork medallions.

Serves:4

Pork Tenderloin with Uncle Al's Potatoes

PER SERVING: FAT: 7.4 GRAMS CALORIES: 289

Olive oil cooking spray
1 to 1 1/4 pounds pork tenderloin, cut into 3/4-inch slices
1 large onion, thinly sliced
2 large potatoes, parboiled and sliced into rounds
Salt and freshly ground pepper to taste
4 vinegar cherry peppers (hot or mild), cored, seeded, and thinly sliced
2 tablespoons vinegar from peppers

When I was a kid, all my family lived in one large house—my parents, grandparents, aunts, uncles, and cousins. On Monday nights, my uncle Al, who cooked in an Italian restaurant, was home from work and he would cook for everyone. I have fond memories of these dinners, and this is my low-fat version of the potatoes prepared by Uncle Al.

1. Preheat oven to 375 degrees.
2. Coat a large nonstick skillet with cooking spray.
3. Heat skillet and add pork. Sauté pork, turning, until lightly browned. Transfer pork to an ovenproof casserole and reserve.
4. Add onion and potatoes to skillet and sauté, stirring frequently, for 3 minutes.
5. Add all remaining ingredients to skillet. Cover and cook for 5 minutes.
6. Transfer ingredients from skillet to casserole, covering pork. (Dish may be prepared in advance up to this point.)
7. Cover casserole and place in oven. Bake until all ingredients are heated through, about 15 minutes.
8. Bring casserole to the table and serve.

Serves: 4

Roast Pork with Campari Sauce

Per serving: Fat: 9.5 grams Calories: 279

Olive oil cooking spray
2 pork tenderloins (about 12 ounces each)
2 shallots, thinly sliced
1/2 cup orange juice
1 tablespoon Dijon mustard
2 tablespoons Campari
1 tablespoon orange zest

1. Preheat oven to 375 degrees.
2. Coat a nonstick baking pan with cooking spray.
3. Place meat in baking pan and roast until a meat thermometer reaches 160 degrees, or until meat is cooked through, about 25 to 35 minutes.
4. Remove meat from oven and keep warm.
5. Coat a saucepan with cooking spray. Add shallots and sauté, stirring, for 1 minute.
6. Add juice and mustard and bring to a simmer. Cook for 3 minutes.
7. Stir in Campari and orange zest and cook for an additional 2 minutes.
8. Slice meat and arrange on a platter. Spoon sauce over meat and serve.

Serves: 4

Ginger Pork with Pineapple and Vegetables

PER SERVING: FAT: 6.8 GRAMS CALORIES: 272

Vegetable oil cooking spray
1 pound pork tenderloin, cubed
2 tablespoons minced ginger
2 small onions, quartered
2 garlic cloves, minced
2 medium carrots, minced
1 green bell pepper, thinly sliced
1/2 pound snow peas
1/2 cup FAT-FREE CHICKEN BROTH (page 52)
1/2 cup canned pineapple chunks with juice
3 tablespoons light soy sauce
1 teaspoon white wine vinegar
1/2 teaspoon crushed red pepper flakes
2 tablespoons cornstarch
1/2 cup water

1. Coat a large nonstick skillet with cooking spray. Heat skillet.
2. Add pork and brown lightly, turning frequently.
3. Add ginger, onion, garlic, carrots, bell pepper, and snow peas. Sauté over low heat for 2 minutes, stirring frequently.
4. Add broth. Drain juice from pineapple and reserve pineapple. Add pineapple juice, soy sauce, vinegar, and red pepper flakes. Cook for 5 minutes.
5. Combine cornstarch and water. Mix thoroughly. Add to skillet and stir to combine.
6. Add pineapple chunks to skillet and continue cooking just until sauce thickens.
7. Transfer ingredients from skillet to a large serving platter and serve with rice.

Serves: 4

Pork Ragout with Fennel in Cream Sauce

PER SERVING: FAT: 6.8 GRAMS CALORIES: 229

1 pound pork tenderloin, cut into ½-inch strips
All-purpose flour
Vegetable oil cooking spray
1 large onion, sliced
3 stalks celery, sliced
4 garlic cloves
1 tablespoon ground fennel seed
Salt and freshly ground pepper to taste
1 cup dry white wine or FAT-FREE CHICKEN BROTH (page 52)
1 tablespoon lemon juice
½ cup nonfat sour cream

1. Lightly coat pork with flour, shaking off excess.
2. Coat a large, nonstick skillet with cooking spray and heat skillet.
3. Add pork and brown lightly, turning frequently.
4. Add all remaining ingredients except for lemon juice and sour cream and cover. Cook over medium-low heat for 30 minutes.
5. Stir in lemon juice and sour cream. Mix to combine and heat through, being careful not to allow sauce to boil.
6. Transfer to a large platter and serve, or spoon over wide noodles before serving.

Serves: 4

Chapter Nine

SIDE DISHES

HERE ARE THE VEGETABLES, salads, and relishes that round out a meal. There are a whole bunch of potato recipes in this chapter—including dishes that you wouldn't believe could be low-fat, but are!

You might combine two or three side dishes to create a delicious main course that's satisfying and healthy, too.

It's best to buy vegetables when they are fresh and in season. Never overcook them, but as in pasta, prepare them *al dente*. An overcooked vegetable loses flavor, color, and vitamins.

Apple and Cranberry Chutney

PER SERVING (1/4 CUP): FAT: 0.2 GRAM CALORIES: 96

6 large Granny Smith apples, peeled, cored, and chopped (about 6 cups)
4 cups cranberries
1 1/2 cups brown sugar, or to taste
2 green bell peppers, chopped
3/4 cup cider vinegar
3/4 cup water
3/4 cup golden raisins
1 medium onion, chopped
1 tablespoon grated ginger
3 garlic cloves, finely chopped

Here's an easily prepared chutney that's wonderful with some of the pork tenderloin dishes. It's also great with chicken. Refrigerate chutney after it has cooled and transfer to jars. Chutney will keep, refrigerated, for about 2 weeks.

1. Combine all ingredients in a large, heavy pot. Mix well and bring to a boil.
2. Reduce heat and simmer, uncovered, for 30 minutes, stirring often.
3. Allow chutney to cool and spoon into jars with covers.
4. Store in refrigerator until needed.

   Yield: About 3 pints

Arugula and Orange Salad

PER SERVING: FAT: 0.3 GRAM CALORIES: 80

3 tablespoons balsamic vinegar
2 tablespoons orange juice
1 teaspoon honey
1 teaspoon Dijon mustard
Salt and freshly ground pepper to taste
2 bunches arugula, wash, trimmed, and dried
2 seedless oranges
2 small red onions, thinly sliced
1 tablespoon orange zest

1. Combine vinegar, juice, honey, mustard, and seasonings in a screw-top jar. Close tightly and shake until all ingredients are thoroughly mixed. Reserve.
2. Tear arugula into bite-size pieces and place in a bowl.
3. Peel oranges. Cut oranges into thin, horizontal slices, and cut each slice into quarters.
4. Add orange, onion, and zest to arugula. Toss.
5. Shake dressing in jar to mix ingredients and pour over arugula mixture. Toss and serve.

Serves: 4

Tangy Sweet-and-Sour Cabbage

PER SERVING: FAT: 0.4 GRAM CALORIES: 56

Vegetable oil cooking spray
1 small onion, thinly sliced
2 garlic cloves, pressed
2 cups coarsely shredded red cabbage
2 tablespoons white wine vinegar
1 tablespoon honey
1/2 cup orange juice
1 bay leaf
Salt and freshly ground pepper to taste

1. Coat a nonstick skillet with vegetable oil cooking spray.
2. Add onion and garlic and cook, stirring occasionally, until onions are just translucent.
3. Add cabbage and cover. Cook about 10 minutes, or until cabbage is barely wilted.
4. Add remaining ingredients and cover. Cook until liquid is absorbed and cabbage is completely wilted, about 15 minutes.
5. If there is any remaining liquid, uncover and cook until liquid is absorbed.
6. Remove bay leaf before serving.

Serves: 4

Orange-Glazed Carrots

Per serving: Fat: 0.2 gram Calories: 95

1 pound baby carrots
1/2 cup orange juice
1/4 teaspoon finely chopped ginger
2 tablespoons honey
Salt and freshly ground pepper to taste
1 tablespoon chopped flat, or Italian, parsley

1. Steam carrots until just tender, about 10 minutes.
2. Drain carrots and reserve.
3. Combine orange juice and ginger in a saucepan. Bring to a simmer.
4. Stir in honey and cook until sauce thickens.
5. Add carrots to saucepan. Heat through and season to taste with salt and pepper.
6. Transfer carrots to a serving dish and garnish with parsley.

Serves: 4

Cilantro-Flavored Cucumber Salad

Per serving: Fat: 0.2 gram Calories: 29

4 medium cucumbers
4 shallots, minced
4 scallions, thinly sliced
1/2 cup white wine vinegar
1 tablespoon sugar
Salt and freshly ground pepper to taste
1/2 cup finely chopped cilantro

1. Peel cucumbers. Cut cucumbers in half, lengthwise. Scoop out seeds and cut into thin slices. Transfer to serving bowl.
2. In another bowl combine shallots, scallions, vinegar, sugar, salt, pepper and cilantro. Mix well and pour over cucumbers. Toss to combine.
3. Refrigerate for 30 minutes before serving.

Serves: 8

Crostini with Mushroom Topping

PER SERVING: FAT: 0.7 GRAM CALORIES: 59

Olive oil cooking spray
3/4 pound mushrooms, chopped
3 garlic cloves, chopped
1/4 cup dry white wine
1 teaspoon light soy sauce
1/2 teaspoon oregano
1/4 cup chopped flat, or Italian, parsley
Salt and freshly ground pepper to taste
16 (1/2-inch thick) diagonally cut French or Italian bread slices
2 garlic cloves, cut in half

1. Coat a nonstick skillet with cooking spray.
2. Add mushrooms and cook, stirring occasionally, for 3 minutes.
3. Add garlic and cook for an additional minute.
4. Add wine, soy sauce, and oregano, and continue cooking for 2 minutes.
5. Stir in parsley, salt, and pepper and continue cooking until liquid from mushrooms has been absorbed. Remove from heat and reserve.
6. Preheat oven to 300 degrees.
7. Place bread on a cookie sheet and toast lightly on both sides. Be careful not to let bread burn.
8. Rub garlic halves on 1 side of each slice.
9. Return bread to cookie sheet and spray with cooking spray.
10. Top each bread slice with approximately 1 tablespoon of mushroom mixture and bake until mushroom topping is hot, about 4 to 5 minutes. Serve immediately.

Serves: 8

Lentil Salad

Per serving: Fat: 4.5 grams Calories: 389

2 cups lentils, cooked
1 medium red onion, thinly sliced
1 garlic clove, minced
2 celery stalks, thinly sliced
4 plum tomatoes, diced
1 tablespoon olive oil
Juice of 1/2 lemon
Salt and freshly ground pepper to taste
2 tablespoons chopped flat, or Italian, parsley

1. Combine lentils, onion, garlic, celery, and tomatoes in a salad bowl.
2. Place oil, lemon juice, and seasonings in a jar with a cover. Close tightly and shake until thoroughly blended.
3. Add dressing to salad and toss until all ingredients are combined. Garnish with parsley and refrigerate until chilled. Serve on a bed of lettuce.

Serves: 4

VARIATION: For a complete meal, top lentil salad with cooked shrimp.

Vera's Green Beans with Tomatoes

PER SERVING: FAT: 0.6 GRAM CALORIES: 54

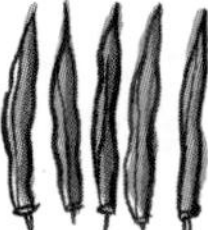

1 pound green beans, trimmed
Olive oil cooking spray
2 garlic cloves, sliced
2 large, very ripe tomatoes, quartered
1/4 cup chopped basil
Salt and freshly ground pepper to taste

1. Blanch green beans in boiling water for 5 minutes. Drain and place colander under cold running water to stop cooking.
2. Coat a nonstick skillet with cooking spray and add garlic. Sauté, stirring, over low heat for 1 minute, being careful not to let garlic burn.
3. Add tomatoes, basil, and seasonings. Mix to combine and cover. Cook for 5 minutes.
4. Stir in green beans and cook for an additional 5 minutes.

Serves: 4

VARIATION: For a heartier dish, add 2 medium parboiled potatoes, cubed, to green beans when you add tomatoes.

Baked Eggplant and Zucchini in Tomato-Basil Sauce

PER SERVING: FAT: 0.6 GRAM CALORIES: 131

1/2 pound nonfat ricotta
Egg substitute equivalent to 1 egg
Salt and freshly ground pepper to taste
1 cup TOMATO-BASIL SAUCE (page 157)
2 Italian eggplant (about 1/2 pound), peeled and sliced lengthwise
1/4 pound nonfat mozzarella, shredded
4 zucchini, thinly sliced
2 teaspoons grated Parmesan cheese

1. Preheat oven to 375 degrees.
2. Combine ricotta and egg substitute in a bowl, add salt and pepper, and mix thoroughly. Reserve.
3. Spread a small amount of sauce in the bottom of an oven-proof casserole.
4. Create layers by alternating eggplant, ricotta mixture, mozzarella, zucchini, and sauce, seasoning to taste. The final layer should be sauce with Parmesan sprinkled on top.
5. Cover casserole and bake for 30 minutes.
6. Allow casserole to rest for 10 minutes before serving.

Serves: 4 to 6

Old-Fashioned Potato Salad

PER SERVING: FAT: 2.2 GRAMS CALORIES: 216

4 medium potatoes, cubed and cooked
1/2 cup low-fat mayonnaise
1/2 cup nonfat sour cream
2 teaspoons Dijon mustard
1 scallion, minced
1 carrot, diced
1 tablespoon white wine vinegar

1. Place potatoes in a serving bowl.
2. Combine all remaining ingredients in another bowl and mix to combine.
3. Spoon dressing over potatoes and toss.
4. Refrigerate for 30 minutes before serving.

Serves: 4

Italian-Style Potato Salad

PER SERVING: FAT: 1.4 GRAMS CALORIES: 163

4 medium baking potatoes, cubed, cooked, and drained
1/2 pound French green beans, cooked al dente
1 teaspoon olive oil
1 tablespoon FAT-FREE CHICKEN BROTH *(page 52)*
2 tablespoons white wine vinegar
Salt and freshly ground pepper to taste
2 tablespoons chopped chives

1. Combine potatoes and green beans in a serving bowl.
2. Place oil, broth, vinegar, and seasonings in a jar. Close tightly and shake until blended.
3. Add chives to bowl.
4. Spoon dressing gradually over all, tossing ingredients as you add dressing. Serve at room temperature or chilled.

Serves: 4

Marylou's Low-Fat Home Fries

PER SERVING: FAT: 0.5 GRAM CALORIES: 162

Vegetable oil cooking spray
4 large potatoes, cooked and sliced
1 large onion, sliced
Salt and freshly ground pepper to taste
Paprika for garnish

1. Coat a large nonstick skillet with cooking spray. Heat skillet.
2. Add potatoes and onion and cook over medium heat, stirring constantly, and adding salt and pepper while ingredients cook.
3. Cook until potatoes are browned on all sides. Transfer to a platter. Garnish with paprika.
4. Serve with meat, fish, or eggs.

   Serves: 4 to 6, unless Jack Nicholson comes to your house for dinner; then it will serve 2.

VARIATION: This is Marylou's recipe, but when I make these potatoes, I add either Vera's peppers, which are hot Italian peppers preserved in oil, or chopped, hot vinegar peppers.

Guilt-Free Gratin of Potatoes

PER SERVING: FAT: 1.4 GRAMS CALORIES: 222

4 medium russet potatoes, thinly sliced
4 small onions, thinly sliced
Salt and freshly ground pepper to taste
2 cups FAT-FREE CHICKEN BROTH (page 52)
1 garlic clove, pressed
1/4 cup minced flat, or Italian, parsley
1/2 cup homemade bread crumbs
1 tablespoon grated Parmesan cheese
Olive oil cooking spray

1. Preheat oven to 325 degrees.
2. In a nonstick baking dish, layer potatoes and onions. Season with salt and pepper and add broth.
3. Bake potato-onion combination for 30 minutes.
4. Combine garlic, parsley, crumbs, and Parmesan cheese. Mix well and sprinkle over potato-onion combination.
5. Spray lightly with cooking spray.
6. Bake an additional 30 minutes.

Serves: 4

Layered Potatoes

PER SERVING: FAT: 0.4 GRAM CALORIES: 192

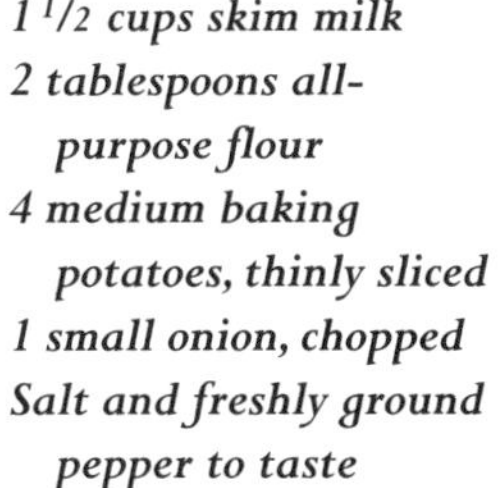

$1\ 1/2$ cups skim milk
2 tablespoons all-purpose flour
4 medium baking potatoes, thinly sliced
1 small onion, chopped
Salt and freshly ground pepper to taste

1. Preheat oven to 375 degrees.
2. Combine milk and flour and mix until blended.
3. Place half the potato slices in a nonstick baking dish. Top with half the onion, season to taste, and pour on half the milk mixture.
4. Repeat with remaining ingredients.
5. Cover dish with foil and bake for 30 minutes.
6. Remove foil and bake for an additional 30 minutes or until potatoes are tender.

Serves: 4

WELCOME BACK MASHED POTATOES!

I think mashed potatoes are everyone's favorite comfort food, and I developed a couple of ways of preparing them without butter or cream. Substitute FAT-FREE CHICKEN BROTH **(page 52) and skim milk for the rich stuff.**

Or mash potatoes with skim milk, nonfat plain yogurt, and a touch of Dijon mustard.

To make sure that the potatoes are lump-free, mash in a saucepan over very low heat, and add salt and pepper to taste.

And how about mashed sweet potatoes for Thanksgiving or whenever you feel like eating sweet potatoes? (Which should be often, because sweet potatoes are loaded with that good beta-carotene stuff.)

Mash those sweets or yams with orange juice, a touch of cardamom, and about 2 drops of maple syrup per potato. You'll love the low-fat results!

Uncle Al's Potatoes II

PER SERVING: FAT: 0.5 GRAM CALORIES: 161

Olive oil cooking spray
1 large onion, thinly sliced
4 medium potatoes, parboiled, sliced into rounds
Salt and freshly ground pepper to taste
6 vinegar cherry peppers (hot or mild), cored, seeded, and thinly sliced
4 tablespoons vinegar from peppers

My Uncle Al's potatoes go with almost every dish and can be served any time: breakfast, brunch, lunch, dinner—whenever! When Uncle Al prepared his potatoes, he made sure to cook them in plenty of oil, but I discovered that parboiled, the potatoes need nothing more than an olive oil cooking spray. Made this way, every bit of the flavor shines through without the fat or calories from excess oil.

1. Coat a large nonstick skillet with cooking spray.
2. Add onion and potatoes to skillet and sauté, stirring frequently, for 3 minutes.
3. Add all remaining ingredients to skillet. Cover and cook until potatoes are tender, all ingredients are heated through, and flavors are combined, about 30 minutes.

Serves: 4

Chicken Stir-Fried Rice

PER SERVING: FAT: 2.2 GRAMS CALORIES: 280

Vegetable oil cooking spray
1 medium onion, finely chopped
1/2 pound boneless, skinless breast of chicken, cut into strips
1/4 pound sliced mushrooms or 1 cup button mushrooms
2 cups cooked rice
Egg substitute equal to 2 eggs, lightly beaten
2 plum tomatoes, chopped
4 scallions, finely chopped
1 cup shelled peas
1 tablespoon light soy sauce
1/2 teaspoon sesame oil
Salt and freshly ground pepper to taste

1. Coat a large, nonstick skillet with cooking spray.
2. Add onion and sauté for 1 minute.
3. Add chicken and continue sautéing until meat is cooked through.
4. Stir in mushrooms and add rice.
5. Add egg and continue stirring until eggs have set.
6. Add tomatoes, scallions, and peas and sauté for an additional 2 minutes.
7. Add all remaining ingredients and stir to combine.
8. Cook for 2 minutes before serving.

Serves: 4

VARIATION: Strips of pork may be substituted for chicken.

Red New Potatoes in Chicken Broth

PER SERVING: FAT: 0.3 GRAM CALORIES: 155

8 small Red Bliss new potatoes, peeled
2 cups FAT-FREE CHICKEN BROTH *(page 52)*
Salt and freshly ground pepper to taste
1/4 cup chopped flat, or Italian, parsley

1. Combine potatoes, broth, and seasonings in a saucepan. Cover and bring to a boil.
2. Reduce heat to a simmer. Cook until potatoes are tender and broth has been absorbed.
3. Transfer to a serving bowl and garnish with parsley.

Serves: 4

Cherry Tomato and Onion Salad

PER SERVING: FAT: 1.3 GRAMS CALORIES: 40

1 pint cherry tomatoes, cut in half
1/4 teaspoon sugar
1/2 teaspoon Dijon mustard
1 teaspoon olive oil
1 tablespoon balsamic vinegar
1 red onion, thinly sliced
Salt and freshly ground pepper to taste

1. Place tomatoes in a bowl. Sprinkle with sugar and toss gently. Allow tomatoes to marinate for 5 minutes.
2. Combine mustard, oil, and vinegar in a screw-top jar. Close jar tightly and shake until ingredients are thoroughly blended.
3. Add onion to tomatoes.
4. Add dressing and toss to combine. Season to taste.

Serves: 4

Baby Peas and Rice

PER SERVING: FAT: 0.8 GRAM CALORIES: 243

Vegetable oil cooking spray
4 scallions, chopped
1 cup rice
2 1/2 cups FAT-FREE CHICKEN BROTH *(page 52)*
1 10-ounce package frozen baby peas, thawed
Salt and freshly ground pepper to taste
2 tablespoons chopped flat, or Italian, parsley

1. Coat a saucepan or skillet with cooking spray.
2. Add scallions and sauté, stirring, for 1 minute.
3. Add rice and broth. Stir to combine. Cover saucepan and cook over medium-low heat for 15 minutes. Add peas and cook until liquid is absorbed and rice is tender. If rice is not tender, add 1 to 2 tablespoons of water.
4. Season to taste and stir in parsley.

Serves: 4

ADD A HOT TOUCH . . .

My mother, Vera, preserves hot Italian peppers in olive oil, and she makes sure I always have a supply. Jack often asks for Vera's peppers, and when I want to add a quick, spicy touch to a meal, I cut up a pepper and distribute the pieces over pasta, chicken, or fish. I'm not suggesting that you use peppers in oil, because even though I do my best to blot off as much oil as possible, there's always some oil permeating the flesh of the peppers. Here's a good substitute for Vera's peppers: use vinegar cherry peppers instead. You'll achieve that hot, piquant flavor without the fat and calories.

Baked Pita Triangles for Dips

PER SERVING (ONE TRIANGLE): FAT: 0.4 GRAM CALORIES: 43

4 pita breads
Olive oil cooking spray
Garlic powder to taste

1. Preheat oven to 400 degrees.
2. Cut each pita bread into 4 triangles.
3. Spray triangles with cooking spray and season with garlic powder.
4. Place triangles on a cookie sheet and bake until crisp, about 15 minutes.

Yield: 16 pita triangles

VARIATIONS: Grated Parmesan cheese, salt, sesame seeds, and poppy seeds are additional options.

Polenta

Per serving: Fat: 1.3 grams Calories: 162

3 cups FAT-FREE CHICKEN BROTH *(page 52), vegetable broth, or water*
2 teaspoons salt (optional)
1 cup polenta (yellow cornmeal)
2 tablespoons grated Parmesan cheese

To prevent polenta from sticking, I cook it in a double boiler. Start out by bringing water to a boil in the bottom part of a double boiler, and then add cooking liquid to upper part of double boiler and continue with the recipe.

1. Bring water to a boil in bottom part of double boiler.
2. Heat liquid to a boil in top half of double boiler. Add salt.
3. Reduce heat to a simmer and add polenta in a stream, gradually, stirring constantly.
4. Stir polenta as it cooks with a wooden spoon.
5. Cook until polenta thickens and pulls away from sides of pot, about 20 to 30 minutes.
6. Stir in Parmesan cheese and serve with chicken, mushrooms, or grilled vegetables.*

Serves: 4

*Polenta does not have to be served immediately. It can be kept warm or reheated in a double boiler.

Chapter Ten

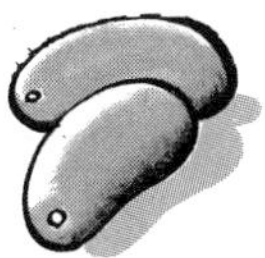

SAUCES

THIS COULD HAVE BEEN the world's shortest book—limited to just one page. That's because the TOMATO-BASIL SAUCE I, on page 157, is Jack's favorite sauce, and spooned over spaghetti, his favorite dish—something he'd be happy to eat every day—maybe twice a day.

The sauce is great, but just in case you don't want to eat the same thing every day, here are a variety of sauce recipes to enjoy with pasta, shellfish, chicken, and meat.

All of them are low in fat, but loaded with flavor from interesting herbs and spices.

Why There Are Three Versions of Red Bell Pepper Sauce

Marylou and I and the chef in Marylou's restaurant all have our favorite way of preparing red bell pepper sauce. You'll find my version—fusilli with red bell pepper sauce I—on page 82. Marylou's—fusilli with red bell pepper sauce II—is on page 83. The chef's version is on page 153.

But whichever version you decide to prepare, all require roasted peppers, so here's how you do that.

Roasted Red Bell Peppers

PER SERVING: FAT: 0.1 GRAM CALORIES: 20

1. Preheat oven to broil.
2. Place peppers on a broiler pan in a single layer and broil. Turn peppers from side to side until they are charred.
3. Place peppers in a paper bag. Close bag tightly and allow peppers to cool.
4. When peppers are cool enough to handle, scrape off charred skin. This is most easily done under cold running water.
5. Core and seed peppers and continue with recipe.

In addition to the recipes here that call for red bell pepper sauce, these sauces can be used on pasta, fish, or shellfish and as a dip for raw vegetables.

Red Bell Pepper Sauce III

PER SERVING (1/4 CUP): FAT: 1.2 GRAMS CALORIES: 40

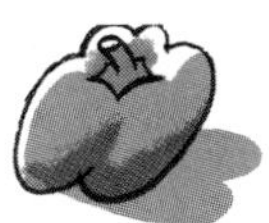

2 red bell peppers, roasted, cut into quarters
2 garlic cloves
1 tablespoon white wine vinegar
1/4 cup orange juice
1/4 cup dry white wine
1 teaspoon olive oil

1. Place all ingredients in a food processor and puree.
2. Transfer puree to a saucepan and cook over low heat until sauce has thickened.

Yield: About 1 cup

Mustard Dill Sauce

PER SERVING (1/4 CUP): FAT: 0.01 GRAM CALORIES: 48

1 cup nonfat sour cream
2 tablespoons Dijon mustard
2 tablespoons chopped dill

This sauce is great with salmon and other fish.

1. Combine all ingredients in a bowl and mix thoroughly.
2. Refrigerate until chilled.

Yield: Approximately 1 cup

Cranberry-Orange Sauce

PER SERVING (1/4 CUP): FAT: 0.1 GRAM CALORIES: 76

1 16-ounce can whole cranberry sauce
1 large, seedless navel orange, peeled and chopped, with juice

1. Combine ingredients in a bowl and mix thoroughly.
2. Cover and chill before serving.

Yield: About 2 1/2 cups

Corn Salsa

PER SERVING (1/4 CUP): FAT: 0.9 GRAM CALORIES: 44

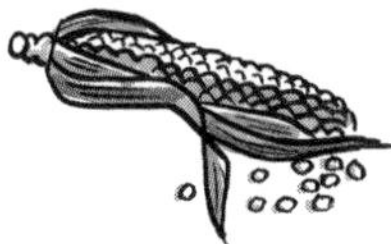

1 10-ounce package frozen corn kernels, thawed
1 medium red bell pepper, diced
2 celery stalks, diced
3 scallions, diced
1 garlic clove, pressed
1/2 medium jalapeño pepper, seeded and minced
1 tablespoon flat, or Italian, parsley, minced
1 tablespoon cilantro, minced
2 tablespoons balsamic vinegar
1 teaspoon olive oil
Salt and freshly ground pepper to taste

1. Combine all ingredients in a bowl. Mix thoroughly and refrigerate for 30 minutes before serving. Corn salsa is delicious served with crab cakes or grilled shrimp.

Yield: About 2 cups

NOTE: Corn salsa may be prepared one day in advance. The flavors will meld and increase while the salsa is refrigerated.

Warm Horseradish Cream Sauce

PER SERVING (1/4 CUP): FAT: 0.01 GRAM CALORIES: 37

1 tablespoon prepared horseradish
1 cup nonfat sour cream
1 scallion, minced
1 1/2 tablespoons lemon juice
2 tablespoons grated lemon peel
1/4 teaspoon salt (optional)

1. Combine all ingredients in a small saucepan.
2. Mix until thoroughly combined.
3. Warm over very low heat. Do not allow sauce to come to a simmer.
4. Transfer to a bowl or sauce boat and serve as a dip with crudités or as a sauce with seafood.

Yield: About 1 1/4 cups

Onion Sauce

PER SERVING (1/4 CUP): FAT: 0.1 GRAM CALORIES: 54

1 large red onion, thinly sliced
1 large yellow onion, thinly sliced
1/2 cup balsamic vinegar
2 tablespoons honey

1. Combine all ingredients in a heavy saucepan. Bring to a boil.
2. Lower heat and simmer, uncovered, for 20 minutes.
3. Transfer to a bowl and refrigerate until chilled. Serve with chicken or pork.

Yield: About 1 1/2 cups

Citrus Vinaigrette

PER SERVING (ONE TABLESPOON): FAT: 0.2 GRAM CALORIES: 7

4 shallots, minced
2 tablespoons chopped basil
1 tablespoon grated orange rind
2 teaspoons grated lemon rind
1/2 cup white wine vinegar
1/4 cup orange juice
3 tablespoons lemon juice
1 teaspoon olive oil
Salt and freshly ground pepper to taste

1. Combine all ingredients in a bowl. Mix until thoroughly blended. Refrigerate until needed.

Yield: About 1 1/4 cups

Orange Mint Sauce

PER SERVING (1/4 CUP): FAT: 0.9 GRAM CALORIES: 35

1 small onion, quartered
1/2 cup orange juice
5 tablespoons lemon juice
1 teaspoon olive oil
2 tablespoons orange zest
1/2 cup packed mint leaves
1/2 cup packed basil leaves
Salt and freshly ground pepper to taste

1. Combine all ingredients in a food processor or blender and process or blend until ingredients are thoroughly pureed.
2. Transfer to a bowl or sauce boat, chill if you wish, and serve with grilled fish—wonderful with salmon—or grilled chicken.

Yield: Approximately 1 1/2 cups

Tomato-Basil Sauce I

PER SERVING (1/4 CUP): FAT: 0.3 GRAM CALORIES: 26

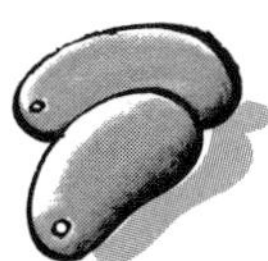

Olive oil cooking spray
1 small onion, thinly sliced
1 small carrot, grated
2 garlic cloves, chopped
1 32-ounce can Italian plum tomatoes
1/4 cup dry red wine
1/2 teaspoon crushed red pepper flakes (optional)
Salt and freshly ground pepper to taste
2 tablespoons chopped basil

The following three sauces differ slightly in that Sauce II calls for tomato paste and Sauce III uses ricotta. I recommend Sauce II when adding meat. Jack's favorite is Sauce I.

1. Coat a large nonstick saucepan with cooking spray.
2. Add onion and carrot and sauté, stirring, for 2 minutes.
3. Add garlic and sauté for an additional minute.
4. Add juice from canned tomatoes and wine and bring to a simmer over low heat.
5. While sauce heats, cut each plum tomato in half and rinse away seeds under cold, running water.
6. Cut tomatoes into strips and add to saucepan.
7. Stir in seasonings. Cover and cook for 20 minutes.
8. Stir in basil.

Yield: About 3 cups

Tomato-Basil Sauce II

PER SERVING ($^1/_4$ CUP): FAT: 0.2 GRAM CALORIES: 18

Olive oil cooking spray
1 small onion, thinly sliced
1 small carrot, grated
2 garlic cloves, chopped
1 2-ounce can tomato paste
1 cup water
1 32-ounce can Italian plum tomatoes
$^1/_4$ cup dry red wine
$^1/_2$ teaspoon crushed red pepper flakes (optional)
Salt and freshly ground pepper to taste
2 tablespoons chopped basil

1. Coat a large, nonstick saucepan with cooking spray.
2. Add onion and carrot and sauté, stirring, for 2 minutes.
3. Add garlic and sauté for an additional minute.
4. Add tomato paste and cook over low heat, stirring frequently, for 3 minutes.
5. Add water gradually and continue stirring until water is incorporated into paste.
6. Add juice from canned tomatoes and wine and bring to a simmer over low heat.
7. While sauce heats, cut each plum tomato in half and rinse away seeds under cold running water.
8. Cut tomatoes into strips and add to saucepan.
9. Stir in seasonings. Cover and cook for 1 $^1/_2$ hours over low heat, adding water 2 tablespoons at a time if sauce becomes too thick.
10. Stir in basil.

Yield: About 4 $^1/_2$ cups

Tomato-Basil Sauce III
Light Tomato Sauce

PER SERVING (1/4 CUP): FAT: 0.3 GRAM CALORIES: 27

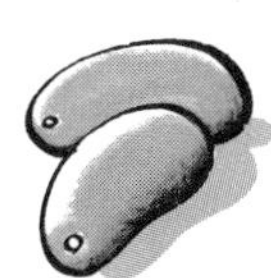

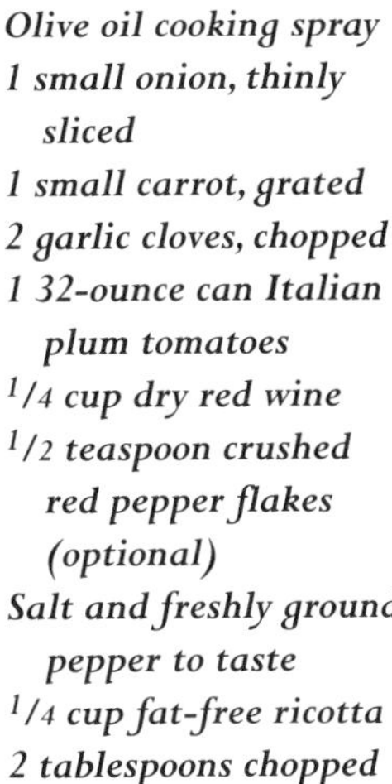

Olive oil cooking spray
1 small onion, thinly sliced
1 small carrot, grated
2 garlic cloves, chopped
1 32-ounce can Italian plum tomatoes
1/4 cup dry red wine
1/2 teaspoon crushed red pepper flakes (optional)
Salt and freshly ground pepper to taste
1/4 cup fat-free ricotta
2 tablespoons chopped basil

1. Coat a large, nonstick saucepan with cooking spray.
2. Add onion and carrot and sauté, stirring, for 2 minutes.
3. Add garlic and sauté for an additional minute.
4. Add juice from canned tomatoes and wine and bring to a simmer over low heat.
5. While sauce heats, cut each plum tomato in half and rinse away seeds under cold running water.
6. Cut tomatoes into strips and add to saucepan.
7. Stir in seasonings. Cover and cook for 20 minutes.
8. Stir in ricotta and heat through. Add basil and stir.

Yield: About 3 cups

Low-Fat Pesto

PER SERVING ($^1/_4$ CUP): FAT: 2.3 GRAMS CALORIES: 50

1 cup packed basil leaves
1 teaspoon pine nuts
2 garlic cloves, cut in half
$^1/_4$ cup lemon juice
$^1/_4$ cup FAT-FREE CHICKEN BROTH (page 52)
1 teaspoon olive oil
1 tablespoon grated Parmesan cheese
Salt and freshly ground pepper to taste

1. In a food processor combine all ingredients and process until finely pureed.
2. Transfer pesto to a jar or bowl and correct seasoning. Refrigerate until needed.

Yield: About 1 cup

QUICK PASTA SAUCES

A lot of the time I have to whip up a fast meal when I have no plans to do any cooking at all. I'm sure this happens to you, too. Here's what I do:

I spray a nonstick skillet with olive oil cooking spray. I chop up a garlic clove or two, add it to the skillet, and sprinkle in a few crushed red pepper flakes. Meanwhile, I put a big pot of water on to boil. When the water comes to a boil I throw in whatever vegetables I have in the kitchen—that could be broccoli rabe, or broccoli florets, or maybe cauliflower—also separated into florets. I might add mustard greens or some of those real skinny French green beans—whatever. I blanch the vegetables for a few minutes, and then remove them from the pot with a slotted spoon.

I add these blanched vegetables to the skillet with maybe half a cup or so of FAT-FREE CHICKEN BROTH (page 52) I stir the whole thing up and cover the skillet.

I add salt to the water in which the vegetables have cooked and then the pasta. The water flavors the pasta nicely. I cook the pasta until it is firm to the bite—*al dente.* I then drain the pasta and add it to the skillet. And finally, a little salt, freshly ground pepper, and maybe a little grated Parmesan cheese. There you have it! Lunch or dinner, or a late-night supper.

Spinach Salsa

PER SERVING ($^1/_4$ CUP): FAT: 1.7 GRAMS CALORIES: 30

1 pound spinach, washed, trimmed, and coarsely chopped
2 garlic cloves, cut in half
2 teaspoons pine nuts
1 teaspoon olive oil
$^1/_2$ teaspoon lemon juice
Salt and freshly ground pepper to taste
1 tablespoon grated Parmesan cheese

1. Place all ingredients, except for seasonings and cheese, in a food processor.
2. Process until smooth and transfer to a bowl. Season to taste and stir in cheese. Mix thoroughly.
3. Serve over pasta, as a dip with vegetables, or as a sauce with seafood.

Yield: About 1 $^1/_2$ cups

Watercress-Yogurt Sauce

PER SERVING ($^1/_4$ CUP): FAT: 0.1 GRAM CALORIES: 32

1 bunch watercress, trimmed
4 scallions, quartered
1 cup nonfat plain yogurt
2 tablespoons apple or orange juice
1 tablespoon white wine vinegar
2 teaspoons Dijon mustard

This sauce also makes a wonderful salad dressing.

1. Combine all ingredients in a food processor and puree.
2. Spoon sauce into a bowl or sauce boat and refrigerate for 30 minutes before serving.

Yield: Approximately 1$^1/_2$ cups

Chapter Eleven

DESSERTS

WE WERE NEVER SERVED overly sweet desserts when we were growing up. My mother would place a colorful pottery platter or bowl on the table, brimming with fruits in season. Then she would peel each of our favorites—Marylou liked oranges in the winter and peaches in the summer, while I ate pears and nectarines. The biggest treat was picking the ripe figs from the tree in our backyard.

The best desserts still are fresh fruits, and if you like fresh fruit with something added, you'll find plenty of good ideas in this chapter. I think the ORANGES WITH AMARETTO (page 168) are elegant enough for a dinner party and are especially refreshing after a meal such as pork tenderloin or lasagna.

There are also pudding recipes, and a Nicholson favorite: RICE PUDDING WITH RAISINS (page 172).

Cantaloupe in Red Wine Marinade

Per serving: Fat: 0.4 gram Calories: 89

1 medium cantaloupe
1 cup dry red wine

1. Cut a 2-inch slice off the top of the cantaloupe.
2. Scoop out seeds and discard.
3. Pour wine into cantaloupe and cover with top slice.
4. Refrigerate cantaloupe for 8 hours or overnight.
5. Using a melon baller, scoop out melon and transfer to a bowl. Pour wine over melon and serve in wine glasses or dessert dishes. Serve with biscotti or other cookies, if you wish.

Serves: 4

Vanilla Bread Pudding with Apples

Per serving: Fat: 0.8 gram Calories: 124

4 slices white bread, cubed
Vegetable oil cooking spray
2 Granny Smith apples, peeled and diced
2 cups skim milk
Egg substitute equal to 2 eggs
1 teaspoon vanilla extract
1 package vanilla pudding (not instant)
Cinnamon for garnish

1. Preheat oven to 375 degrees.
2. Place bread cubes on a nonstick cookie sheet and coat lightly with spray.
3. Bake until toasted, turning once, about 10 to 15 minutes.
4. Transfer bread to a baking dish and add apples. Stir to combine.
5. Combine milk, egg substitute, and vanilla extract in a large bowl. Whisk until blended.
6. Add vanilla pudding and continue whisking until all ingredients are combined.
7. Spoon pudding mixture over bread and apples.
8. Bake pudding for 30 minutes. Remove from oven and allow pudding to stand for 5 minutes before serving. Sprinkle with cinnamon.

Serves: 8

Apple-Amaretto Crisp

Per serving: Fat: 2.6 grams Calories: 218

Butter cooking spray
4 Granny Smith apples, peeled, cored, and quartered
2 tablespoons sugar
1 1/2 cups Marsala wine
8 amaretto cookies, crushed into crumbs

1. Preheat oven to 350 degrees.
2. Coat a baking dish with cooking spray.
3. Place apples in baking dish and top with sugar.
4. Pour wine over apples and top with crumbs.
5. Lightly coat crumbs with cooking spray.
6. Bake crisp for 45 minutes or until apples are tender and crumbs have browned.

Serves: 4

Melon Mixture with Strawberry Sauce

PER SERVING: FAT: 0.5 GRAM CALORIES: 129

1 medium ripe cantaloupe
1 medium ripe honeydew
3 tablespoons Grand Marnier
1 pint strawberries, hulled and sliced
1/4 cup orange juice
3 tablespoons sugar

1. Using a melon baller, scoop both melons into balls, or cut into bite-size pieces.
2. Place melon balls into a large bowl. Add Grand Marnier and toss.
3. Cover and refrigerate for at least 1 hour.
4. In a food processor or blender, combine strawberries, orange juice, and sugar. Process or blend until smooth.
5. Transfer to a bowl. Cover and refrigerate for at least 1 hour.
6. To serve, spoon melon ball mixture into 8 dessert dishes and top with strawberry sauce.

Serves: 8

Oranges with Amaretto

Per serving: Fat: 1.0 gram Calories: 158

4 large, seedless oranges
1/4 cup amaretto liqueur
1/4 cup orange juice
4 amaretto cookies, crumbled

1. Peel oranges. Cut peel on one orange into julienne strips. Slice oranges horizontally, cutting away membrane.
2. Place oranges on a serving platter and spoon amaretto and orange juice over oranges. Add julienne strips. Turn oranges in liqueur and refrigerate for 30 minutes or longer.
3. Just before serving, sprinkle orange slices with amaretto cookie crumbs.

Serves: 4

Peach Halves in Raspberry Sauce

PER SERVING: FAT: 0.5 GRAM CALORIES: 277

SAUCE

1 pint raspberries or 1 10-ounce package frozen raspberries, thawed
1/4 cup water (if you use fresh raspberries)
1/4 cup superfine sugar
1 teaspoon vanilla extract
2 tablespoons currant jelly
2 tablespoons fruit-flavored liqueur or white rum (optional)

PEACHES

1/2 cup sugar
1 cup water
2 tablespoons lemon juice
4 large, ripe peaches (preferably freestone), peeled, halved, and pitted
4 mint sprigs

SAUCE

1. Combine all ingredients in a food processor. Process until completely smooth.
2. Strain sauce into bowl. Refrigerate until chilled.

Yield: About 1 1/2 cups

PEACHES

1. Combine sugar, water, and lemon juice in a saucepan. Bring to a boil. Reduce heat to a simmer and cook until liquid is syrupy—about 10 minutes. Remove from heat.
2. Place peach halves, cut side down, in a large skillet.
3. Pour syrup over peaches and cover. Poach peaches in syrup for about 5 minutes, or until just tender. Don't overcook, or peaches will fall apart.
4. Remove peaches from syrup, and place 2 peach halves in each dessert dish. Spoon sauce over peaches, and garnish with mint sprigs.

Serves: 4

Here are two versions of a virtually fat-free fruit topping that is delicious over plain cakes, poached fruits, or fat-free plain yogurt.

Raspberry Glaze I

PER SERVING (1/4 CUP): FAT: 0.1 GRAM CALORIES: 95

1 package frozen raspberries in syrup, thawed
1/2 teaspoon unflavored gelatin
2 tablespoons Framboise liqueur or Grand Marnier

1. Place raspberries in a blender or food processor and puree.
2. Strain raspberries and place in a saucepan. Stir in gelatin and liqueur. Simmer over low heat, stirring, until gelatin has melted and combined with fruit.
3. Transfer to a bowl and allow glaze to cool to room temperature before serving.

Yield: About 1 cup

Raspberry Glaze II

PER SERVING (1/4 CUP): FAT: 0.2 GRAM CALORIES: 130

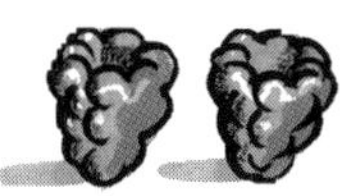

1 package frozen raspberries in syrup, thawed
3 tablespoons apricot jam or currant jelly
2 tablespoons Framboise or apricot liqueur

1. Place raspberries in a blender or food processor and puree.
2. Strain raspberries and return to blender or processor. Add other ingredients and blend thoroughly.
3. Transfer to a bowl and refrigerate until needed.

Yield: About 1 cup

Apricot-Filled Baked Apples

PER SERVING: FAT: 0.7 GRAM CALORIES: 162

4 tablespoons apricot preserves
4 large Granny Smith apples, cored
1 cup apple juice
1 teaspoon cinnamon
1/2 teaspoon nutmeg

1. Preheat oven to 350 degrees.
2. Spoon 1 tablespoon apricot preserves into cored center of each apple.
3. Place apples in a nonstick baking pan.
4. Pour apple juice into pan and sprinkle each apple with cinnamon and nutmeg.
5. Bake for 40 to 50 minutes, or until apples are tender. If you wish, serve apples with fat-free yogurt or fat-free whipped topping.

Serves: 4

Rice Pudding with Raisins

PER SERVING: FAT: 1.1 GRAMS CALORIES: 208

1 1/2 cups skim milk
1/3 cup sugar
1/4 teaspoon salt
1 teaspoon light whipped butter
Egg substitute equal to 4 eggs
1 cup rice, cooked
1/2 cup white raisins, soaked overnight in 1/2 cup white rum (optional)
1 teaspoon vanilla extract
1/4 teaspoon ground nutmeg
Vegetable oil cooking spray
2 teaspoons cinnamon

This rice pudding is deliciously low calorie—skim milk is the answer. Jack likes it with raisins that have been soaked overnight in white rum; however, the pudding is so flavorful that the raisins are optional.

1. Preheat oven to 350 degrees.
2. Combine milk, sugar, salt, and butter in a saucepan. Cook over very low heat until sugar is dissolved and butter has melted. Remove from heat and allow to cool.
3. Place egg substitute in a bowl. Slowly stir in milk mixture.
4. Add rice, raisins, vanilla, and nutmeg. Stir to combine.
5. Lightly coat 6 custard cups or 1 soufflé dish with cooking spray.
6. Spoon rice mixture into cups or soufflé dish. Sprinkle cinnamon on top.
7. Create a bain-marie by placing a roasting pan in the oven and adding water. Allow water to heat and place custard cups or soufflé dish in roasting pan. (Water should come one-third of the way up on cups or soufflé dish.)
8. Bake for 20 to 30 minutes, or until a toothpick inserted near the center of pudding comes out clean. (Test after 20 minutes.)
9. Remove from oven and serve warm or at room temperature. If you wish, serve with RASPBERRY GLAZE (page 170) on the side.

Serves: 6

Index